CLUES TO THE NICENE CREED

CLUES TO THE NICENE CREED

✠   ✠

A Brief Outline of the Faith

David Willis

William B. Eerdmans Publishing Company

Grand Rapids, Michigan / Cambridge, U.K.

© 2005 Wm. B. Eerdmans Publishing Co.

Wm. B. Eerdmans Publishing Co.

255 Jefferson Ave. S.E., Grand Rapids, Mich. 49503 /
P.O. Box 163, Cambridge CB3 9PU U.K.

Printed in the United States of America

10 09 08 07 06 05   07 06 05 05 04 03 02 01

Library of Congress Cataloging in Publication Data

Willis, David (David E.)
Clues to the Nicene Creed: a brief outline of the faith / David Willis.
          p.   cm.
Includes bibliographical references and index.
ISBN 0-8028-2868-X (pbk.: alk. paper)
1. Nicene Creed.   I. Title.

BT999.W55   2005
238′.142 — dc22

2005045112

www.eerdmans.com

To

Elizabeth, Benjamin, Matthew, Catherine

Rebecca, Spencer

and

Laurie, Whitney, William

Contents

✠   ✠

Introduction

✠   ✠

For Whom

This book is for those who would like to be reminded of what they are standing for when they recite the Nicene Creed and would welcome help in distinguishing the few essentials of the faith from the numerous matters of relative indifference.

It happens that men and women are elected to this or that office in a congregation. They take their vows seriously. They feel the need to reexamine what they are affirming — and what they do not have to agree with — in taking on this responsibility. That happens, for example, when someone is being baptized. The godparents, parent or parents, and the whole congregation are making promises to nurture another in the faith. Over coffee after the service, one often hears such comments as "I am glad to help. But, you know, many times I really don't feel I *have a clue* about what I mean when I use some of the words of the creed!"

This short treatment of the creed intends to offer some clues for being startled afresh by the depth and beauty of certain affirmations — and for letting go with a good conscience things that do not belong to the cost of discipleship. I make no pretense to be exhaustive in my treatment of any single portion of the creed's distillation of the faith. Rather, my aim is — as the title suggests — to provide clues for thinking through again the main evangelical truths set forth in the most ecumenical of creeds.[1] It is up to each and every member of the covenanting Christian community continually to think through the meaning of his or her baptism and thereby to keep prepared for her or his form of Christ's ministry.

What

There is a tradition that says believers have a "sense of the church" long before they have a doctrine of it. *Sensing this way is a form of knowing* a reality long before being aware of knowing it. It is like what happens when a person who has grown up in this or that context comes to realize the extent to which it has become part of her or his identity. That is the way many know the creed. *There is a sense of the truth of the creed that predates critical consciousness of its components.* Yes, of course, the intellect is party to this knowing. However, the sensing goes beyond and far precedes cogitation. It is tactile knowing, kinesthetic memory, somatic recognition, soulful wonder, psychic discovery at the deepest level of a person's being. It is what we mean by saying we "know something by heart," though that phrase, unfortunately, has come to mean rote memory. The "heart" properly refers to the whole person,

---

1. For relatively recent studies of the Nicene Creed, see Brian Hebblethwaite, *The Essence of Christianity* (London: SPCK, 1996); Geddes MacGregor, *The Nicene Creed Illumined by Modern Thought* (Grand Rapids: Eerdmans, 1980); Christopher Seitz, ed., *Nicene Christianity* (Grand Rapids: Brazos, 2001); Thomas F. Torrance, ed., *The Incarnation: Ecumenical Studies in the Nicene-Constantinopolitan Creed* (Edinburgh: Handsel Press, 1981); Marianne Micks, *Loving the Questions* (Cambridge, Mass.: Cowley, 1993). Two less recent but fine works are George Forell, *Understanding the Nicene Creed* (Minneapolis: Fortress, 1965), and John Burnaby, *The Belief of Christendom* (London: SPCK, 1975).

the conscious dimensions but also the vastly larger and deeper unconscious domains of the self.

Knowing the creed is of this tactile order of knowing, sensing the reality to which the words of the creed point. Yes, the creed comes in textual form, words written and read, amenable to parsing, grasping the reader with graphic power. However, it is above all in the act of "standing" with other members of the congregation and reciting the creed in response to the proclaimed Word that this sensing of the truth of the creed becomes an event time and time again. I put "standing" in quotes because those who have not the strength to rise, the paralyzed and otherwise infirm, are often the people who best count the cost of confessing the creed. Reaffirming the faith *also* entails conscious assent to the constitutive parts of the creed. The truth of the creed that one senses is, however, *the encountering identity of the living God*, trusting in whom we realize our responsive identity. The truth is the matter of our knowing someone — not so much something as someone — by heart. The resonance of the creed, the sonorous repetition by the company of the equally forgiven sinners, reminds us that our identity is our belonging to that vast company of those down through the ages who have engaged in the costly act of reconfessing the faith. What comes to expression in reciting the creed together is the knowledge that we belong to that glorious society of those who in every age cry, "I believe. Help my unbelief."

On Style

The English translation of the Bible that I will use unless otherwise indicated is the Revised Standard Version. Sometimes I put in brackets the particularly rich words or phrases being translated.

I am one of the multitudes that continue to look for better ways of using inclusive language so that the hearing of the gospel is not impaired by the false scandal of sexist language or by the false scandal of tendentious overcorrection. I know that I succeed in this endeavor as poorly as others. I also know, however, that this is not the time in the life of the church to keep silent in the face of the terrible amnesia we suffer about what it means to confess anew the ancient truths.[2]

This treatment of the creed is an *outline* of the essentials[3] of the Christian faith, so I attempt, with only a modicum of success, to keep footnotes to a minimum. Where I use footnotes, I do so not to expand an argument but to identify sources and to suggest further reading for those so inclined.

2. I use the guidelines on inclusive language developed by the General Assembly of the Presbyterian Church U.S.A., and in this usage I find most helpful the remarks of my friend William C. Placher, in *Jesus the Savior* (Louisville: Westminster John Knox, 2001), pp. 22-32. For a range of feminist preferences, see Maryanne Stevens, ed., *Reconstructing the Christ Symbol: Essays in Feminist Christology* (New York: Paulist, 1993).

3. For others who use the word "essential" to apply to Christian doctrine, see William C. Placher, ed., *Essentials of Christian Theology* (Louisville: Westminster John Knox, 2003), and Hebblethwaite, *The Essence of Christianity*.

CHAPTER ONE

The Earthiness of the Creed

✠   ✠

Graceful Mass and Momentum

In the East Wing of the National Gallery, not far from each other, are a Calder mobile and a Henry Moore pair of bronzes, menhir-like in their depth of mystery. They do not have to mean anything. Rather, they evoke so many responses, and different ones at different times of the day and at different seasons in the lives of those drawn into their power, that they defy being reduced to a narrow range of awe. These works have an almost mystical force to probe and cause to surface deep archetypal longings among people. In this respect they remind me of the glorious material of the Nicene Creed. There is a certain holy bulkiness and mobility to these sculptures which prompt the comparison.

When I refer to "the glorious material" of the creed, I hasten to disown any thought that the material of the creed is an easily controlled, malleable, acquiescent medium. The title of Fernand Pouillon's novel is translated *The Stones of the Abbey,* though the French means the wild stones.[1] The flinty stone, rebellious raw

---

1. Fernand Pouillon, *The Stones of the Abbey* (New York: Harcourt Brace Jovanovich, 1985); French edition: *Les Pierres Sauvages* (Paris: Editions du Seuil, 1964).

material, is what the Cistercian community sticks with. Spirituality is materiality. It is working with the hard matter at the abbey's site instead of importing more amenable limestone. The stubborn material shows; it imposes limits on what the community can build and how it builds. New imagination is demanded. New disciplines are required by the material and the construction.

The material of the creed is like that, often intractable, freeing in its tenacity. In Tillich's terms, the symbols which give the community its identity have their own power and their loaded times.[2] They grasp, take hold of, exert their power and beauty and judging precision in a quickening process. The sane believer knows the wisdom of always being exposed to this angular material. The material shapes him or her. That is because the Subject to whom the symbols point and in which they really participate is the Encountering One ultimately identified by Jesus the Christ. The glory of this material is exactly its victorious ungloriousness, its humility, its sovereign servanthood. It is, in other words, the cross of the risen Lord, Jesus the Christ.[3] The material is *scandalon:* stumbling block, stone that trips us up and sends us staggering in another direction than before. We become differently inclined, tilted with different penchants than before. This matter sets us off balance and resets us toward a new equilibrium.

This is not unlike the dynamics of architecture. An obtuse malpractice has crept into some contemporary theologians who

2. For Tillich's treatment of the *kairoi* of symbols, see Paul Tillich, *The Protestant Era* (Chicago: University of Chicago Press, 1953), pp. 13-15, 32-51.

3. On the theology of the cross, see Reinhold Bernhardt and David Willis, "Theologia Crucis," in *Evangelisches Kirchenlexikon,* ed. E. Fahlbusch et al. (Göttingen: Vandenhoeck & Ruprecht, 1996), vol. 7, cols. 734-36; Gerhard O. Forde, "Luther's Theology of the Cross," in *Christian Dogmatics,* ed. C. Braaten and R. Jenson (Philadelphia: Fortress, 1984), 1:47-63; Alister McGrath, *Luther's Theology of the Cross* (Oxford: Blackwell, 1985); Jürgen Moltmann, *The Crucified God* (New York: Harper and Row, 1974).

set structure or foundational over against dynamic and openness, associating the latter with organic (lively) terms and the former with static (and lifeless) terms. While I am sympathetic with their intention, they quite miss the point that a well-designed and constructed edifice is a lively, quick thing:[4] a structural instance of what Karl Menninger called the *vital balance*.[5] There is something like a vital balance in stonecrafting that uses the recalcitrant materials of life to soar to other dimensions of life, to comfort, to delight, to protect. An arch looks simple when in place and when successfully upholding other interdependent parts of the whole, but its very strength and simplicity result from painstaking shaping and placing of individual stones — often at considerable peril to the builders. Even if we did not have the apostolic switch from one analogy to another, we would know what it means to speak of "living stone."

Comparing the material of the creed to Calder's mobile is no less apt: unity of mass in motion, astral turning of new tensions, equivalence known even when countervailing parts are not seen, light shifting with earthy revolutions, energy expanding in trajectoral grace. Were the mobile units crystal, we would be caught up in shifting frequencies of the color spectrum: unseen light accommodating to become visible, hidden brilliance filtered through crystal, refraction in slow dance of luminary speed. We need receiving surfaces to see the moving frequencies. Integral to the comparison is having receptive responders, reflecting surfaces, which are light seen in the light of light.

4. For Cistercian spirituality and construction, see Francis Evans, "The Engineer Monks," in *A Definitive History of Abbey Dore*, ed. Ron Shoesmith and Ruth Richardson (Little Logaston Woonton Almeley, Herefordshire: Logaston Press, 1997), pp. 139-48.

5. Karl Menninger, *The Vital Balance* (New York: Viking Press, 1963).

Holy Writ and the Rule of Faith

Not every congregation has a place for the creed in its worship and church ordering. Indeed, it is argued by some that, for all practical purposes, the creed becomes a substitute for the Scriptures; and if not exactly a substitute, then at least a superfluous reduction of the biblical messages. That objection can be voiced by two otherwise contrary views of Scripture: (a) that the whole of the Bible is literally true, the revelation so completely given that subsequent elucidations are not only unnecessary but misleading; and (b) that the biblical material and the creedal summaries are early but superseded stages of religious development of which any given cultural expression is as valid as any other. There is some truth to both objections in the sense that they are reminders of twin dangers: either thinking revelation is exhausted by any single cultural expression of God's presence, or thinking that we can minimize the radical particularity of the God witnessed to in the Old and New Testaments.

Those in creedal traditions variously insist that the creed is a highly selective concentration of the main truths of the Bible, Old Testament and New. It is a definitive, not exhaustive, summary of the affirmations used at baptisms to identify the God whose love is to be trusted above all and to identify the people created by the call of that God. That call is the Word of God to a nonpeople and makes them into a people, the Word that gives an identity to those otherwise without one. The written form of the Word of God — the Scriptures of the Old and New Testaments — has an authority second only to the eternal Word of God above all revealed in Jesus Christ by the power of the Holy Spirit. The authority of the creed is secondary to the authority of Scriptures and serves to enhance the right reading, the informed passion, which those Scriptures themselves evoke.

The Scriptures have authority not because they are some hypothetical data bank of literally true facts, say of ancient Middle East cosmology. The Scriptures have authority because of their calling power, because God uses them by speaking through them by the power of the Spirit to call people time and time again, throughout the centuries and into the future, to hear God's word and so recall their identity as God's servant people. As word of God, the Scriptures call forth that trusting knowledge that is faith, a doxological summary of which is the creed.

The creed in this sense was as squeezed out of people as was the Shema, Israel: "Hear, O Israel! . . ." Confronted by a threat to the very identity and continuity of right worship of the living God, the people, in both cases, hear a call and reply with a re-hearsal of God's saving nature and acts. In both cases the people bear witness to what has happened to them at the hand of this God. As new threats to the gospel truth arose, especially as the distilled baptismal vows are translated in a new context, the church found that it *had to expand the creed* — in order, in the face of new threats, *not to say less than the truth*. One of the creed's functions is to guard against reductions. The creed helps keep together those things that belong to the complementary range of biblical messages. It serves as a help in the right reading of the Scriptures and in the right proclamation — the spoken form of the Word of God — which arises out of them.

This relative but real authority of the creed is reflected in some orders of worship practiced by many congregations who take seriously their place in a creedal tradition.[6] I mention three implications of the creed's place in these liturgies.

---

6. See Iain Torrance and Bryan Spinks, eds., *To Glorify God: Essays on Modern Reformed Liturgy* (Edinburgh: T. & T. Clark, 1999); and the influential German Rites of Strasburg, in William D. Maxwell, *An Outline of Christian Worship: Its Development and Forms* (London: Oxford University Press, 1952), pp. 87-111; Joint Committee on Worship, *The Worshipbook: Services* (Philadelphia: Westminster, 1970).

First, the worshiping context reinforces the praise-giving nature of the creed. Yes, we critically examine the creed and test its wording, and, yes, we identify those places where this or that confusion might arise. But that very examination is an action of doxology: we praise God no less with our minds and critical questions than with our hearts and resounding affirmations. For example, it is difficult and pointless not to sing the cadences the Nicene Creed uses to point to Christ's identity: ". . . God of God, Light of Light, true God of true God, begotten not made, of one being with the Father. Through him all things were made. For us and our salvation. . . ." The language is at the same time precisely tough and inescapably joyful.

Second, in the liturgy the congregation stands to recite the creed after the readings of Holy Writ and after proclamation based on those texts. That means that the creed was and remains a response to the written and proclaimed forms through which God chooses to address the Word to us.

Third, in the liturgy the creed is a link between the proclamation and the prayers of intercession. Intercession brings with it a commitment to act on behalf of those being prayed for. That commitment includes serving "all sorts and conditions" of humans, not just believers, and all God's creation, not just the human part of it. The congregation that is gathered by the Word knows itself to be also those who are dispersed by the Word into every corner of life. The congregation that stands for the creed knows it stands alongside of, and often in the place of, those for whom it prays. Intercession is not worrying condescension. Intercession also includes a petition not just to help others but also to open ourselves to be helped by others whether or not they are believers, others whom we also need to respect and hear, others who address us with a prophetic word of repentance and assurance of pardon.

The Most Ecumenical Creed and Others

Out of the many versions of the earliest baptismal confessions of faith, several main forms of the creed emerged.[7] The best-known and most widely used were the so-called Apostles' Creed and the so-called Nicene Creed (381). While both are accepted in most of the churches in the creedal tradition, the one most widely accepted in the West and the East was the creed approved by the Third Ecumenical Council held at Constantinople in 381. It reflects more of the doctrinal development of the third and fourth centuries than does the Apostles' Creed. The latter has its own beauty and concentrated punch, its own selectivity, its own pedagogical usefulness. These two ancient creeds so reinforce and amplify each other that when people recite one, the wording of the other is always coaching in the background.

I will say something later about the complementarity of different views of baptism, but here we are dealing especially with the connection between baptism and the Nicene Creed. The creed grew out of much shorter statements of commitment when people chose to be baptized — or to have their household baptized. In that act they were sticking out their necks, endangering their worldly goods and lives and those of their household,

7. On the development of the several creeds, see J. N. D. Kelly, *Early Christian Creeds* (London: Longmans, Green and Co., 1950); J. N. D. Kelly, *Early Christian Doctrine* (New York: Harper and Bros., 1958); Jaroslav Pelikan, *The Christian Tradition*, vol. 1, *The Emergence of the Catholic Tradition (100-600)* (Chicago: University of Chicago Press, 1971); Bernhard Lohse, *A Short History of Christian Doctrine* (Philadelphia: Fortress, 1966), especially chaps. 1–3; Robert Jenson, "The Nicene-Constantinopolitan Dogma," in *Christian Dogmatics*, vol. 1, chap. 2, second locus; and William C. Placher, *A History of Christian Theology* (Philadelphia: Westminster, 1983). On the philosophical material on which this development drew, see Diogenes Allen, *Philosophy for Understanding Theology* (Atlanta: John Knox, 1985), and Gerhard Ebeling, *The Study of Theology* (Philadelphia: Fortress, 1978), chap. 5, "The Partnership of Theology and Philosophy."

joining what we today would probably call an underground movement — a movement forced underground by the authorities who considered the confession that Jesus Christ is Lord a seditious stance.

Though we use the term "baptism" today more often than not, there was a good point to the old parlance wherein the act was called "Christening." For in baptism one takes on the name of Christ, gets named as one belonging to that ragtag, hot and cold, rich and poor, healthy and sick, cussed and blessed community to whom Christ has united himself by the power of the Holy Spirit. The church is all those people who get stuck with each other in Christ, like it or not, in season and out, through thick and through thin, past, present, and future. Read Bonhoeffer's *Life Together* again.[8] He has this gloriously gritty business of community well documented, prophetically, lovingly — and he knew the community reached out to include his jailers.[9]

The nub of the baptismal formula was simple enough: "Jesus Christ, Lord," but the consequences of the existence of the community willing to live and die by this confession were world shattering. The main struggle was over whether there were an Old and a New Testament, which meant whether there was a community of believers in Jesus who were in continuity with the people whose struggles and hopes and experiences are the material of the Hebrew Scriptures, the canonical writings sacred to Israel. New writings proved to be the most hope-sustaining in those communities that under persecution could make stick their claim to continuity with the original apostles and that used the "rule of faith" in baptisms. These eventually came to be recognized as the canonical writings of the New Testament. The succinct baptismal vows

8. Dietrich Bonhoeffer, *Life Together* (New York: Harper, 1954).
9. See Eberhard Bethge, *Dietrich Bonhoeffer* (New York: Harper and Row, 1970).

served to focus the identity of that community whose freeing loyalty was to Jesus the Jewish Messiah, the Lord of the whole universe. This Jesus of Nazareth is the long-awaited Jewish Messiah, Anointed One, Christ. That claim is scandalous enough. Add to that, however, that he is the crucified, risen, and vindicated Lord of the whole creation, the one who will return to judge the living and the dead. The additions to the Nicene Creed over the years were made because not to say more in the face of threats to this claim would be to compromise its scandalous simplicity.

In the face of dilutions and misleading interpretations, the church had to say more in order not to say less than what is inherently implied in the simplest baptismal confessions. What was implicit becomes explicit in this doctrinal development, especially, but not exclusively, to 381. The Nicene Creed is *not* what Tillich would call authority imposed from the outside and over which Christians ought not to argue.[10] The creed has authority as believers stand for it, as they stand against some other claims and practices that are contrary to the love of the Triune there confessed. Whenever the creed was used — as indeed it later came sometimes to be — to bully people into conforming to a state religion, its nature as a free covenanting act of reowning, reclaiming for oneself this form and content of the faith, its true nature, was tragically debased. I think, for example, of the use of the sword to try to quell many of the movements within what has come to be known as the Radical Reformation, though such forceful repression had been already going on for centuries.[11] Yet the creed is part of the way the gospel gets passed on. Something occurs when I am so moved by the gospel mediated through members of

---

10. See Tillich's treatment of "heteronomous authority" in *Systematic Theology*, 3 vols. (Chicago: University of Chicago Press, 1951-63), 1:83-86.

11. See the diversity treated in George H. Williams, *The Radical Reformation* (Philadelphia: Westminster, 1962).

the body of Christ that I decide to throw my lot in with those who identify themselves by standing up for the creed and for the One to whom it points. We believe it and rejoice in it. We critically study the creed, but what we are studying essentially belongs to the liturgy and is to be sung with the other voices around us.

One of the things we learn from the creed is the humanness of the church's faith. In a subsequent chapter I say something about the dangers of what one can call "appearance Christology." Its more formal name is Docetism, from the Greek word meaning "to appear." By whatever name, it is the view that Christ was divine but *only appeared to be human.* The idea is that the humanness gets in the way of the divinity. It is an attitude that shows up in many things. For example, sometimes people seem to think that the less human, say, the Scriptures are, the more divine they are and thus supposedly the more authoritative. The Christian faith, however, is a historically mediated faith. The church's humanity is one of its essential aspects. When we say that Christ came for us and for our salvation, and that the Mediator was tempted in all points as we are but did not sin, and it is a true saying worthy of all belief that Christ came into the world to save sinners, we are remembering that the living God is the one free enough, loving enough, powerful enough to become incarnate of the virgin Mary. One of the strengths, and not one of the weaknesses, of the creed is that it is the product of — so the believer confesses — a whole series of events and pressures which, while not what the creed can be reduced to, nonetheless played an indispensable part in its growth. The creed's earthiness is one of the most important truths it teaches us, we whose humanity is divinely intended.

The Nicene Creed has a relative standing under Scripture and alongside other creeds, ancient and modern. I have said something about its relation to the other main ancient creed, the Apostles' Creed. Another is worth mentioning, namely, the so-called

Athanasian Creed.[12] It never gained the ecumenical acceptance that the others did, though as a commentary on the Nicene Creed it is quite valuable. It is a good example of the way the Nicene Creed teaches matters that need clarification, restatement in subsequent contexts and with changing terminology — exactly as a result of what the creed teaches. That is, it belongs to the very dynamics of the creed that it invites restatement in subsequent contexts, invites fundamentally new translations and reinterpretation — not to diminish the truths of the creed but to render its claims compelling and intelligible in successive cultures. Their contextualization belongs to the very nature of the truths confessed in the Nicene Creed. The route of inquiry sometimes goes from a later to an earlier formulation. Old actions of faith acquire new meanings. In this study I will sometimes draw on subsequent confessions to help understand what is at stake in the creed.

Subsequent confessions and local creeds are articulated to deal with challenges to the church's faith from without and within. The subsequent confessions of faith are like midcourse corrections necessary to move forward along the trajectory set early on. Some traditions have compiled books of confession or books of concord to show that the later confessions of faith[13] move in the direction and with the momentum set by the most ecumenical of the creeds. Other traditions get at the forward-moving nature of the Nicene Creed by embracing changes in the liturgical context in which it is resung and reaffirmed.

---

12. J. N. D. Kelly, *The Athanasian Creed* (New York: Harper and Row, 1965).

13. Like the Thirty-nine Articles, the Augsburg Confession, the Heidelberg Catechism, the Barmen Confession, the Confession of Korea, the Confession of the South African Bruderbund, or in a different genre, the historic Plan of Union of the Church of South India. For various recent Reformed documents, see Lukas Vischer, ed., *Reformed Witness Today: A Collection of Confessions and Statements of Faith Issued by Reformed Churches* (Bern: Evangelische Arbeitsstelle Oekumene Schweiz, 1982).

The relative brevity, even sparseness, of the creed is part of its point. It is a richer symbol for its saying the bare essentials. Like the marriage vows, or the three-line mystery of the faith we proclaim in the Eucharist, more is connoted by less. Simplicity is the opposite of oversimplification, the opposite of just cutting out indiscriminatingly. Simplicity is the result of intense, disciplined, tenacious selectivity. There is a silence that is informed response to radical simplicity. Such silence is the result of disciplined letting go of the superfluous. This kind of minimalism was practiced long before the term was used. There seems to be a cross-culture recognition of it. It is striking, for example, in a Zen rock garden or a flower arrangement of one stalk. The stark simplicity, the compelling brevity, evokes meditation. In the case of the creed, the sacred symbols are long meditated upon and come to overt expression in the act of reciting the faith and taking on its cost.

Much is deliberately left to the imagination, for the imagination is one of the most important corresponding realities that the creed quickens in the believer. We are, by it, moved to a different image of self in relation to others. There is an iconic power to the creed's radical selectivity. The depth of mystery grasps us, moves us to awe, has a freeing power over us. It is an aesthetic shock of recognition, but one that is at the same time awe in the presence of the holy. As such, it redefines beauty to include the wondrous hunger for justice.

Essentials and Flourishes

The Nicene Creed is not a set of propositions a person has to assent to or else. The "or else" contains the threat that such and such dire consequences, like going to hell, will result from a person's refusal or inability to assent to an external authority. Assenting to something and following certain rules out of threat is one of the things Paul means by living by the law rather than living by the gospel.[14] That is because the gospel means good news — is another name for good news. Good news quickens a person, moves a person to delight in the changes it announces.

One of the things that makes credible the all-inclusive good news of God's relentless love is that it is true whether or not we accept it. Its not being dependent on our acceptance of it is one of the good features of the good news, one of the things that makes us wholeheartedly embrace it. Compelled love is not the real thing. Compelled assent to the creed, grudgingly dutiful compliance to it as a dogmatic law, is the opposite of the passionately informed trust, the quickened response to the gospel, which is the very nature of the faith of the church. We are not saved by our own faith or our own righteousness; we are moved by the free gift of God's love to sing the wondrous things God has done and does. That's what it means to experience wholeness by the grace of God, and that applies also to that part of our wholeness that is doctrinal specificity.[15]

Calvin's distinctions on this are helpful. He pointed to what he called the three parts of Christian freedom: freedom from works righteousness, freedom to practice the Decalogue, and freedom to be indifferent about indifferent things.[16] It is the latter which most interests us in this section. It is one thing to know that we do not earn wholeness by assenting to the creed. It is a second thing to grow in understanding the creed that we freely embrace. It is a third thing to practice sorting out those things that are essential from those that do not amount to much and are certainly

14. For the law-gospel relationship, see Gerhard Forde, "Eleventh Locus: Christian Life," in Braaten and Jenson, eds., *Christian Dogmatics,* vol. 2.

15. Recall the old hymn "There Is a Wideness in God's Mercy." In the first, last, and intervening places, the latitude of human compassion is a variation of the wideness of divine love.

16. John Calvin, *Institutes of the Christian Religion* 3.19.

not worth rejecting one another over. Love distinguishes between the necessary and the superfluous. Love does not stubbornly insist on indifferent things as if they were at the core of mutual trust.

One of the functions of the creed for those free to embrace it is that it helps them distinguish between those beliefs that belong to the core of the faith and those that are, by comparison, peripheral. The use of this distinction comes from that philosophical tradition known as Stoicism, according to which happiness came with toning down one's expectations. A wise indifference, a seasoned apathy, results from cultivating a detachment from worldly encumbrances. It is easy to see how some forms of spirituality could make use of Stoicism to devalue life in this world. While it bears some similarities to this view, being indifferent about indifferent things has a distinct function when understood as the third part of Christian freedom. This world is good because it was made by a good God and is to be enjoyed. The danger comes when a person makes anything other than God the focus of security and happiness. The creed helps keep this sane focus, helps sort out the few things worth one's life. It is like a filter which cuts static way back so you can hear the central message more clearly. The selectivity is not to communicate less; it is to communicate more of the reality being pointed to.

The creed is a canonical summary, a summary of what shapes my conscious and unconscious praise and thanksgiving, just as the "Shema, Israel" is recited to remind Israel of her identity and to refocus her praise and recommitment.[17] Its very antiquity is part of the point. In standing up for the creed and standing up for what it stands for, I am accepting my place in the long procession moving forward from the past that belongs to God into the future that belongs to God. I see in my mind's eye the procession lining the up-

---

17. On the formation of the "Shema Israel," see John Bright, *A History of Israel*, 3rd ed. (Philadelphia: Westminster, 1981).

per reaches of St. Apollinare-in-Classe — the glorious mosaics — with each more-than-life-sized figure gazing forward at the unmistakably victorious Christ. When you look back at these figures, you are swung around by their gaze to focus on the coming one, after whose appearance, looking for another is superfluous.[18]

The Faith and Other Faiths

The faith of the church is one among many faiths. Their respective truth claims and ethical systems have often been complementary. Today we are seeing, however, a reassertion of sectarian conflict at a time when living together on a global scale is more imperative than ever. Dialogue among the faiths is a necessity, not an interesting option. That includes the dialogue partners being as clear as possible about the bases of their respective truth claims and about their motivations for listening attentively to each other. That is quite different from discounting all truth claims made by whatever religion or claiming that all are saying the same thing without knowing it — which, of course, is a truth claim itself.[19]

One of the blessings of a workable separation between church and state is that a person is free to profess the creed or not. A person will not lose civil status if he or she chooses not even to pay lip service to it. For the first three centuries after Christ's epiphany, the church was a severely persecuted minority. When the emperor be-

---

18. I also see in my mind's eye the procession Mrs. Turpin has a vision of at the end of Flannery O'Connor's short story "Revelation." Flannery O'Connor, *The Complete Stories* (New York: Farrar, Straus and Giroux, 1972).

19. One of the most helpful models for the encounter of world religions and quasi religions remains Tillich's Columbia University lectures: Paul Tillich, *Christianity and the Encounter of the World Religions* (New York: Columbia University Press, 1964). On the senses of "religion" and "religions," see also Ebeling, *The Study of Theology,* chap. 4.

came a Christian and considered the church an instrument to help prevent the empire from splitting apart, all that changed. As the faith spread among immigrating people who then came to consider themselves part of Christendom, it became increasingly difficult to draw the line between being baptized and being a good citizen of the state. Even after the breakup of the Holy Roman Empire and the end of medieval society, the Christian religion was so favored in some circles that unless a person was at least a nominal Christian, he or she was in effect socially ostracized. Today that situation, for the most part, no longer obtains.

The same cannot be said, ironically enough, of those places in the world suffering from a resurgence of intolerant forms of other religions. In some areas, being a Christian is as dangerous as it was before Christianity ever became a state religion. Even — some would say, especially — where Christians have made an easy peace with the surrounding secular culture, it is clear that the believing community lives in an alien environment. The scandalous claims of the gospel and the unavoidable cost of discipleship make confessing the creed an act of witting risk. The freedom to confess the faith comes with the choice to go against the stream. That is an analysis of hope, not of grudging acceptance, for it means the joyful practice of membership in the age-long communion of the saints.

There is an ephemeral *so-called tolerance* born of intellectual lassitude and cynical passivity. There is, however, a *substantive tolerance* that is a respectful curiosity about the richness other faiths have to offer. This *intrigued humility* is often a matter of aesthetic discernment. What we call tolerance is often a fond admiration for what we see in this or that person whose religion may be quite different from ours. This substantive tolerance is the opposite of insulting condescension. It entails spontaneous approbation; but it also entails a critical realism about the wrongs in each religion that need correcting. That includes the prophetic criteria by which to recognize beliefs and practices needing reform and the loving procedures to carry out reform.

Standing up for what you believe is an act of faith, and a costly one at that. In our secularized society the obvious sounds harsh: Christians count on different things being true than non-Christians do. That obviously does not of itself make them better people than others, though ultimately there is a behavioral connection between the love the believing community haltingly struggles to practice and costly grace active in service. It is just that here, as in most relationships, boundaries are important: identities are not just interchangeable parts. Genuine pluralism means that I respect other viewpoints and guard their right to be heard in dialogues from which all parties learn something not realized before. This genuine pluralism means that I am free to insist as much on my convictions as I expect others to insist on theirs. Humility, that seemingly much-maligned quality, is foundational to genuine pluralism. It means that I acknowledge that I have unimagined truth to learn from other traditions — and that others and I have unimagined truth to learn from forebears in my own, Christian, tradition.[20]

Each religion claims to have the resources for such growth and reform. In the case of Christianity, the fundamental motivations and procedures for such a prophetic affirmation are implicit in the creed. When the creed speaks of Christ as the light and the Eternal Word by whom all things are made, it is drawing on the vision of the prologue to John's Gospel.[21] According to that, Jesus

20. Many of the issues touched on here are helpfully discussed in Miroslav Volf, "Theology, Meaning and Power: A Conversation with George Lindbeck on Theology and the Nature of Christian Difference," in *The Nature of Confession,* ed. Timothy R. Phillips and Dennis L. Okholm (Downers Grove, Ill.: InterVarsity, 1996), pp. 45-56.

21. Tillich sees the prologue to John's Gospel as the basis of an inclusive view in the encounter among religions and quasi religions, but he points out that

is the same one who is the light which illumines all people, whose incarnation is the way we know the universality and quality, including forgiveness, of the love God wills for all creation.[22] The movement is from radical concreteness to universal conclusions, from security in one's freely given identity to affirming the particular identity of others. One of the tasks of this present study is to spell out a bit more what this creedal movement from concreteness to universality looks like.

As for me and my household — those who speak out of their own convictions — the Nicene Creed is of immense use in confirming time and time again the identity given me and that I reaccept as my own. It helps me remember who I am in relation to others, to remember a sense of self in relation to others who may well embrace a quite different identity. It is part of my own conviction that the God I know in Christ has an inclusive love for all creatures, often and long unbeknownst to them. How the Holy Triune chooses to be accommodated, transfigured, through other religions is quite beyond my prescriptions; but I do know that there is a reason we say not only that God loves but that the God we know in Christ is love. The particularity of the confession of faith made in the creed includes openness to the place of other religions in the divine economy.

---

there is, even in the prologue, material which could — and did — become exclusionist: that is why Tillich calls for dialogue rather than conversion as the aim of such encounter. Note the importance of the word "encounter," for it means that each religion or quasi religion brings a strong sense of its concreteness, a healthy sense of self, to the process.

22. A rereading of the early Christian apologists, like Justin Martyr, is in order. They sought, with the tools they had, to insist on the unity of truth wherever it appeared and sought to ground truth's unity in the omnipresence of the divine Word which had become incarnate as Jesus Christ. See H. R. Niebuhr's typology for them in *Christ and Culture* (New York: Harper Torchbooks, 1956).

CHAPTER TWO

What Believing Means

✠   ✠

We believe in God . . .

Carriers of the Faith

It is a toss-up whether to begin the Nicene Creed with "I believe in God . . ." or "We believe in God . . ." Both usages are ancient.[1] The first-person singular emphasizes the fact that the individual believer is making a personal recommitment, though even then it is as a member of the body of Christ that the individual speaks. The first-person plural emphasizes the fact that confessing the creed is part of Christian life together, though even then the common voice is made up of the sounds of individuals exchanging the

---

1. For different versions of the creed, see Philip Schaff, *Creeds of Christendom* (Grand Rapids: Baker, 1966). In early liturgies the catechumen's profession of faith was made before the baptism and its wording was kept secret from those not of the Christian community. See Josef A. Jungmann, *The Early Liturgy* (Notre Dame, Ind.: University of Notre Dame Press, 1959), chaps. 7 and 8. The rudimentary creed was brief, more like the Apostles' Creed than the fuller Nicene-Constantinopolitan Creed that we are using in this study and that takes account of the debates of the third and fourth centuries.

peace. I will use both, but I have a preference for saying "We believe." Doing so reminds me that even in the seasons when I am wobbly on this or that part of the creed, I am sustained by the realization that it is normal to rely on others who, as it were, believe on my behalf, just as they may from time to time rely on my believing on their behalf. Such vicarious trust works, of course, only because it is based on Christ's fidelity and the intercessory reality of the Holy Spirit.

Before we say more about the carriers of the faith, those through whom we come to faith, we need to note that the opening words are "We believe *in God* . . . ," not just "We believe" or even "We believe in." That is because believing is not primarily about our believing. Otherwise it would be like focusing on a lens instead of looking through the lens at the subject focused on.

God's presence and activity are such that we are moved to *informed trust* in God. God's presence and activity are what bring forth and define what we call believing. It is not informed trust to believe primarily in ourselves, much less in our believing. That would be misinformed trust. Faith is not religious narcissism. Moreover, we say "We believe *in* . . ." because in the first instance believing is *entrusting* the loving God who encounters us. Yes, of course, we also say we believe *that* such and such is the case. We say we believe this or that to be true. *Believing that* is also part of faith.[2] Even so, the contents of faith result from the trustworthiness of the one who stands behind his Word. More on this later. Now we turn to the carriers of faith.

Remember the friends in the story in Luke 5:17-26. They can-

2. Cf. George Lindbeck, *The Nature of Doctrine* (Philadelphia: Westminster, 1984), and Avery Dulles, *The Assurance of Things Hoped For: A Theology of Christian Faith* (New York: Oxford University Press, 1994), and Alexander J. McKelway, "The Logic of Faith," in *Toward the Future of Reformed Theology*, ed. David Willis and Michael Welker (Grand Rapids: Eerdmans, 1999); and Alexander Schmemann, *I Believe . . .* (Crestwood, N.Y.: St. Vladimir's Seminary Press, 1995).

not get close to Jesus because of the crowd around him. So they climb on top of the house, dig a hole in the roof, and lower their paralyzed friend, cot and all, into Jesus' presence. The rest of the story is startling. Jesus addresses the cripple with words that could appear to change the subject but actually go to the heart of the matter: "Man, your sins are forgiven." The Pharisees are quite understandably shocked: "Who is this that speaks blasphemies? Who can forgive sins but God only?" The drama is heightened when Jesus replies to their questioning: "'Which is easier — to say "Your sins are forgiven you" or to say "Rise and walk"? But that you may know that the Son of man has authority on earth to forgive sins . . . ,' he said to the man who was paralyzed, 'I say to you "Rise, take up your bed and go home."' And immediately he rose before them, and took up that on which he lay, and went home, glorifying God. And amazement seized them all, and they glorified God and were filled with awe, saying, 'We have seen strange things today.'"[3]

This was a miracle in the strict sense. It was a sign of the presence of the kingdom: only God can forgive sins; Jesus forgives sins and in doing so heals the cripple; so draw your own conclusion. What I want to call attention to, however, is the presupposition behind Christ's addressing the paralytic. That presupposition is the action of those friends who were determined that their friend be brought into Jesus' presence. It was thus then and it is so now: the individual's movement from paralysis to cot-carrying mobility presupposes those who are insistent enough to bring him or her, at unroofing determination, into the crowd around Jesus. So it was then and is now: the individual believes because someone has brought him or her into the range of the gospel. The individual's own variant faith is just that: a variation on the faith of those who

---

3. I have tried this punctuation, different from that used in the RSV, to try to show the pace with which this dialogue and its consequences move along.

trusted enough to make a fuss until out of the conflict came a new freedom and richness of life.

That is one side of the coin, namely, that our faith presupposes the faith of the community which transmits the gospel generation after generation, and in doing so continually reinterprets it so new hearers can actually hear the good news in their own contexts and tongues. The other side of the coin is just as important, namely, that each and every member of God's household has a particular take on the formative hopes, identifying narratives, normative sets of trusts of the believing community.

Each person is like a prism through which light is refracted with slight or great variation, and each pattern of refracted light belongs to the evolving fullness of the community's life. Or, the shape, color, placement of the tiles in a Byzantine mosaic confront us with an ensemble which is the reflected texture of holiness. To be whole, each member of the community needs the particularity of each other member, no matter how distant or close in time and geography. That is the fundamental reason for the ministry of listening to one another, of taking the time and exercising the imagination — and patience — with each other to respect and learn from each other dimensions and nuances of the gospel which we would not, could not, embrace on our own. "That would not have occurred to me," we say when a mediated insight befalls us. This is dynamic catholicity, of which, more later. The Holy Spirit is continually at work guiding and deepening our experience of the manifold effulgence of the faith once received and always renewed.

The Knowledgeable Leap

Much has been made of "the leap of faith." As a protest against the complacent illusion of absolute certainty before taking any stand, the image of faith as a leap is a healthy correction. Or as a protest against a passionless acquiescence in what one may have grown up with but never critically examined, the insight that faith entails a radical risk is surely accurate. Still again, when a person leaps from one context into another, there is a certain note of irreversibility to the choice. One's life is forever different. There is a before and an after, and the after is costlier than the before.

Yet faith is not a blind leap into the void, an assertive will to believe. Faith is an act of daring gamble based on the best chances made apparent by the cumulative experience of God's trustworthiness. Faith is a calculated risk, a decision to embrace life often in the face of contradictory evidence but still an *act of informed trust*. It is indeed a risk, in the sense of Pascal's wager.[4] It is quite possible that death, destruction, and cruelty are the dominant realities; but when all is said and done, life is better lived if one thinks and acts as if ultimately grace triumphs. The odds are not equal, and, in any event, betting on sovereign grace is the way of a daring life.

Faith is not an absence of knowledge, not what one has instead of knowledge, as is often implied in a loose manner of speaking. It is a common mistake to think of faith being on one side of a teeter-totter and knowledge on the other side: more faith — less knowledge, more knowledge — less faith. As Calvin so crisply puts it, faith is not "ignorance tempered by humility."[5]

---

4. Pascal's wager is described in *pensée* 451: Blaise Pascal, *The Pensees* (Baltimore: Penguin Books, 1961), pp. 155-59.

5. Calvin, *Institutes of the Christian Religion,* ed. J. T. McNeill, trans. F. L. Battles, 2 vols. (Philadelphia: Westminster, 1960), 3.2.3. See the previous paragraph (3.2.2): "Faith rests not on ignorance, but on knowledge. And this is, indeed, knowledge not only of God but of the divine will. We do not obtain salvation either because we are prepared to embrace as true whatever the church has prescribed, or because we turn over to it the task of inquiring and knowing. But we do so when we know that God is our merciful Father, because of reconciliation

Rather, faith is a particular kind of *knowledge*. It is a risk-taking kind of knowing, and as such the kind of knowing apt to matters of ultimate concern. It is the kind of knowledge entailed in human creativity, in choosing life of redefined abundance. It is a kind of knowledge that helps us have a better understanding of other kinds of knowledge. But it, faith, is a committed, engaged, passionate *knowledge* of God's *benevolence* toward us — *even* toward us. That is what Luther keeps insisting on: faith grasps that the gospel is a *"for us" fact.*[6]

One of the best definitions of faith, one worth committing to memory, is Calvin's. "Now we shall possess a right definition of faith if we call it a firm and certain knowledge of God's benevolence towards us, founded upon the truth of the freely given promise in Christ, both revealed to our minds and sealed upon our hearts through the Holy Spirit."[7]

Such knowledge is not, in today's parlance, "a head trip." Such knowledge (again, Calvin's words) is not that which "flits about in the brain" *(cerebrum),* but that which "takes root in the heart" *(cor).*[8] Faith is heartfelt knowledge. It is what Calvin calls true piety. "This sense of the powers of God is for us a fit teacher of piety, from which religion is born. I call 'piety' that reverence joined with the love of God which the knowledge of his benefits in-

---

effected through Christ, and that Christ has been given to us as righteousness, sanctification, and life" (p. 545).

6. On Luther's insistence on the *pro nobis,* see Heiko Oberman, *Luther: Man between God and the Devil* (New Haven: Yale University Press, 1989).

7. Calvin, *Institutes* 3.2.7; McNeill ed., p. 551.

8. Cf. Calvin, *Institutes* 1.5.9: "We are called to a knowledge of God: not that knowledge which, content with empty speculation, merely flits in the brain, but that which will be sound and fruitful if we duly perceive it, and if it takes root in the heart. For the Lord manifests himself by his powers, the force of which we feel within ourselves and the benefits of which we enjoy" (McNeill ed., pp. 61, 62). Also, on faith not being religious credulity, "heedless gullibility," see again *Institutes* 3.2.3 (McNeill ed., p. 545).

duces."[9] Faith is knowing by heart the one on whose heart all the members of his body rely. When we feel overwhelmed by doubt, so Bernard observed, we do not feel God to be in our hearts; but that does not mean that God ever ceases to have us *in his heart*.[10] Our faith — as trusting knowledge of God's benevolence — is not faith in our faith, nor heartfelt experience of our experience, and so on.

Faithful Doubt

Above I said that ultimately faith entails a wager that when all is said and done, the divine benevolence is sovereign. "When all is said and done" and "ultimately" are necessary qualifications, qualifications which belong to the core of faith. There are fearful valleys of doubt as well as heights of assurance. The full gamut belongs to faith. We must take care not to minimize the doubt side of the faith of the disciples as narrated in the New Testament. Nor can we avoid their doubt by saying they had only the seed of faith while they doubted. It is a source of comfort to us to be reminded that of those gathered at the ascension, it is reported that "some doubted," and that at Christ's appearance to the disciples after the event on the road to Emmaus, some "disbelieved for joy" (Luke 24:41). Then look at the quieting of the storm (Mark 4:35-41; Matt. 8:23-27; Luke 8:22-25). Who can fail to identify with those of little faith who awakened Jesus? Their awakening Jesus was already an act of faith: they called on the one who, they were convinced, could calm the storm. Yet Christ, in Matthew, says they are of little faith.

9. Calvin, *Institutes* 1.2.1; McNeill ed., p. 41.

10. In *Insitutes* 3.2.25 (McNeill ed., p. 571), Calvin cites Bernard's Fifth Sermon on the Dedication of a Church.

We saw above that Calvin spoke of "a firm and certain knowledge of God's benevolence." He had to explain that he did not thereby mean that faith was not a continual struggle.[11] I do not think, however, that Calvin went far enough in that explanation. In fact, almost as often as not, believers get guided, comforted, compelled, and sustained from day to day by other members of Christ's body. There are times when we are dependent on what I think we must recognize as the *vicarious faith of the community*. Often the community trusts on our behalf. We need to recognize — rejoice in, let ourselves be helped by — that vicarious trust of the community to which we belong, in season and out.

I realize there is a danger in what was called "implicit faith" if by that was meant (as Calvin took it to mean) a substitute for personal faith: not knowing what you believe, abdicating your own informed trust, turning over your own thinking about the faith to this or that expert. Nonetheless, Calvin also had pastoral recourse — partly because he wished to defend infant baptism — to what he called "a seed of faith" that, while not fully grown, was in the disciples (as in their calling on Jesus to quell the storm) and that, while not fully grown, is there, like a mustard seed, in infants of believing parents. Or, to change images (and it is a mixed metaphor, not to be pushed too far) to one Cyprian used and that was also a favorite of Calvin's: the church is the mother without whom we do not have God for our father, the one at whose breast we are nourished and learn from in the *schola Christi*.[12]

All I am insisting on in recognizing the comforting reality of the *vicarious faith of the community* is that since we are united to Christ in his body and since it is finally Christ's own fidelity on which we rely and who is the author and finisher of our faith,

---

11. Calvin, *Institutes* 3.2.15-20; McNeill ed., pp. 561-66.

12. Also on this imagery, see Lukas Vischer, "Church: Mother of Believers," in *Toward the Future of Reformed Theology*.

even in our most forlorn and apparent unbelief we do not fall out of the nexus of sane trust. Reread Peter DeVries' *The Blood of the Lamb*.[13] The father whose daughter has just died of leukemia hurls her untouched birthday cake at the statue of Christ above the door to the sanctuary of St. Jude's next to the hospital. His act is as much one of faith — and a more honest act of faith — than were he to mouth sentimental nonsense couched in supposedly pious terms. And do not miss the point that the father has been engaged in long discussions with the Jewish father of another girl also in the oncology ward. There, in that setting and in those actions, the people of God are present and are faithful in ways appropriate to that excruciating context. I intentionally use the word "excruciating," and I know that DeVries knows that St. Jude is the patron saint of apparently lost causes. ·

I have added "apparently" because of the distinction C. S. Lewis and J. R. R. Tolkien[14] draw between (a) the pagan teaching about "tragic ending" (an inbuilt flaw coming to an inevitable conclusion) and (b) recognizing that some of the most dreadful endings are to be seen as "*eu*catastrophes," good culminations undreamed of in the midst of the trials. Part of the foolishness, the scandal, of the gospel is the idea that catastrophes are not the end in themselves but are material which eventually will be reshaped to some, now unimagined, good. The good news includes the belief that ultimately, no matter how far away and with what unimagined twist, the only inevitable thing is sovereign love.

13. Peter DeVries, *The Blood of the Lamb* (Harmondsworth: Penguin Books, 1982).

14. In C. S. Lewis, ed., *Essays Presented to Charles Williams* (Grand Rapids: Eerdmans, 1966).

Discovering One's Place in the Story of Jesus

Mark puts the offense of the gospel most sharply. He moves the account along briskly. As he tells it, it is not just those who encounter Jesus who are amazed. Jesus is also astounded. He is amazed at the extent of unbelief among those who are eyewitnesses to his deeds and teaching. When Jesus begins teaching in the synagogue of his home village, those he has grown up with do not know what to make of his teaching and actions.

> "Where did this man get all this? What is the wisdom given to him? What mighty works are wrought by his hands! Is not this the carpenter, the son of Mary and brother of James and Joses and Judas and Simon, and are not his sisters here with us?" And they took offense at him. And Jesus said to them, "A prophet is not without honor, except in his own country, and among his own kin, and in his own house." And he could do no mighty work there, except that he laid his hands upon a few sick people and healed them. And he marveled because of their unbelief.
>
> And he went about among the villages teaching.
>
> And he called to him the twelve, and began to send them out two by two, and gave them authority over the unclean spirits. He charged them to take nothing for their journey except a staff. (Mark 6:2b-8a)

The presence of Jesus the Christ creates the deepest crisis: decision is demanded about what is to be made of this man. We cannot escape that question if we are to know the radical humility of the Messiah's presence. This side of the cross and resurrection and Pentecost and the shaping of the church, it is often difficult to hear the story of Jesus in its personal concreteness. Pilgrimages to the Holy Land were taken by people who, among other things, were hungry for this sense of immediacy: whatever else Jesus was and is, he walked along the same road I am walking along, he saw the same configuration of hills I see when I look up, he and his followers stopped near here when going from this to that place, and so on. Squabbling about the exact site of this or that event rather misses the main point: that there is a drawing power to the story of Jesus which is an integral part of the reaction God's word quickens in us.

This is part of the way Jesus keeps his promise to be with us to the end of the ages. That quickening, fascinating power of the story has its way with us whether we be men and women of the first, third, ninth, twelfth, sixteenth, nineteenth, twentieth century, and those in between and ahead. There is a pilgrimage quality of allowing oneself to be confronted time and again with the radical ordinariness through which extraordinary new life happens to people around Jesus. What happens to people around Jesus is *amazing*.

Time and again, the Gospels record the first reaction people had to Jesus' presence and actions: "And they were *amazed*." Or, as we saw at the conclusion of the story in Luke about the healing of the paralytic: "And amazement seized them all, and they glorified God and were filled with awe, saying, 'We have seen strange things today'" (Luke 5:26). Amazement was and is a large component of faith. Amazement is asking the question, how could this be happening? It asks, did I really see what I thought I saw, really hear what I thought I heard? Is this event really happening to me? Amazement contains an element of incredulity at the utterly unimagined turn of events. We are amazed, even when at one level we may have been told to expect something like this. We find ourselves moved to living ordinary lives in a startlingly different context. We say we are "living in a different world." One cannot be blasé about the story of Jesus. That is partly what is meant by the comparison of the kingdom to children. They are free of the false sophistication that is a defense against getting caught up in the new world that befalls us in the story of Jesus. Whatever else it is, the story of Jesus is amazing in this life-changing sense.

Whatever else it is, faith is amazement at finding ourselves caught up in that story. Below, in another chapter, I will say something about the senses in which Jesus' story is richly composite. I want here only to make the point that believing is the same as accepting the fact of our being part of that canonical story and its inclusive extension. Finding ourselves in the story is another way of describing the dynamics of faith. I mention only three aspects of being caught up in that normative story and so discovering self.

First, being caught up into the normative story is *relocation of self into a larger reality than one knew of before*. It is movement from a more constricting to a more freeing context. Only when that movement occurs does one look back and see the prior context for what it is. The prior context may not have been mainly destructive — though it may have been — but it is seen in retrospection to be a stage on the way to the greater reality — which itself becomes a stage toward even further, unimagined growth. This movement is one of *placement* and *replacement*. There is something to the fact that the Greek verb for "to believe" means to trust *into*. It is discovery of one in whom to *place* trust. We discover our unique place, the unique part we are set apart to play, in the story of Jesus, of being *dislocated* and *relocated*.

The image of the vine (for example, in John 15:1-11) is apt: we are transplanted, engrafted into a larger reality, and we discover self as belonging to the larger reality. Apart from that vine, we soon wither; a part of that vine, we bear the fruits of love. Being engrafted into that vine, discovering self's place in the story of Jesus, is freedom to grow. Faith in this sense can be succinctly defined: acknowledging one's place in the story of Jesus. It is replaced self-knowledge, a discovery of childhood's capacity to discover, a recovering of the wondering self. Perhaps for the first time we come to know we are benevolently known.

Second, being caught up in the normative story is *repeatedly to recognize self in that story*. This is similar to the point of the previous paragraph, yes; but it helps us see that faith is not so much a matter of having this or that — as when people say they "have" or do not "have" faith. Were we, for some reason, to insist on the "having faith" language, it would be more accurate to say that the faith has us, grasps us, possesses us. Or, once again, as the passage in Luke 5 says, they were seized by amazement. We recognize ourselves: in the paralytic walking home, in the woman at the well, in the criminals executed alongside Jesus, in Peter's retreat before the servant girl's spotting him, in those who walked the road to Emmaus with Jesus and recognized him in the breaking of bread, in Thomas's holding out for tangible proof, in those who disbelieved for joy, in the paralytic at the side of the pool of Bethesda, in the lepers healed whether grateful or not, in the un-horsed persecutor of the church, and so on. We "identify" with these persons. The ancient stories apply also to us, to me, centuries later. We lose ourselves in the greater reality and thereby (there are no shortcuts) find ourselves in a vast company of similarly forward-moving women and men.

Third, making that existential link with others in the canonical story is *a gift*. Much can be done and must be done to learn as much as possible about the economic, political, religious, and other dynamics at play in this or that part of the normative story of Jesus. That story is the one leading up to his epiphany, extending through his earthly ministry and forward into the lives of those following him. That is to say that the story of the Bible, Old Testament and New, is that of Jesus, Alpha and Omega. However, not all who study the story of Jesus are moved to an existential recognition of self therein. That discovery, finally, is a free, unmanufactur-able, unpredictable inheritance. It is what the New Testament calls *gift*. In Greek the word for "gift" and "grace" is the same *(charisma)*. As Augustine nicely puts it, faith is called a *gift* because it is a *gift!*

That gift is what is referred to as the secret work of the Holy Spirit. The Spirit takes the things of Christ and applies them to us. The Holy Spirit is the bond by which we are united to Christ. To participate in his story through this gift of existential recognition is to participate in him, to share his destiny, to die with him and to be raised with him, to share his love for others in this beloved old battered world. We will have more to say about this when we examine (a) what it means to say that Christ is both the Mediator and the Subject mediated, and (b) what it means to say that the church is the mystical body of Christ. For now, it suffices to point to the amazing consequences of being grasped by the story of Jesus.

Degrees and Seasons of Faith

The church is called the congregation of believers. That does not mean the church is comprised of people who have already attained what they are counting on. It means that the church is made up of women and men of a gritty trust in a gritty world. The church is the body gathered by the Word and Spirit being led as Israel was in the desert. "I believe; help my unbelief!" (Mark 9:24) is canonical utterance. The church is made up of people who are struggling in faith with the faith, helping others who are doing the same and letting others help them. Faith is part of the community's intercession for each other and the world. Often all a hard-pressed, severely tested person can do is hold fast to the knowledge that his or her "loss of faith" is nothing new to believers and that in the meantime God will not let him or her go whether or not faith is in its waxing or waning rhythms, whether it is a season when doubt dominates or when assurance is in the ascendancy.

Once again here we are confronting a serious misunderstanding about the nature of believing. It is serious not just because it is inaccurate. It is serious because it can deprive people of the guidance and comfort they most need in times of the severest testing. Faith is not a fair-weather joyride for spiritual types. Often as not, faith is a balancing on the brink of despair, holding fast with both hands to God's promises even — perhaps especially — when one cannot articulate that trust. Nor, by the same token, is faith religiously rationalized entitlement to heroic tragedy. Often faith is the experience of integrity, wholeness, peace that defies comparison, even — perhaps especially — when speech seems to trivialize overwhelming happiness. Both extremes miss the point that faith is a continuum of trust that grows, like everything living grows, by season, with waxing and waning, with this idiosyncrasy or that. Moreover, faith grows, ironically enough, by a certain attitude of relaxation, or letting go, detachment. It grows best when it is not continually being uprooted for endless reexamination, a kind of vivisection of one's religious self-consciousness.

What I am saying is rather obvious; but like many supposedly obvious things, its implications can be minimized. The obvious thing is that faith is a developmental reality. Faith remains sane by taking, within a broad range like that of the essentials of the creed, different shapes with different speeds and differing degrees of clarity. There has to be time for a believer to go through a differentiation of self vis-à-vis others, and that differentiation for next proximity belongs to the very nature of maturing faith. There is also a season of reintegration, of consolidation of new insights in a momentum of transforming moments. That is what is behind the beautiful insight of the biblical language: God knows each person by name. The shepherd knows each charge by its own sound. That means more than that God watches over us, though that is marvelously true. It means also that God has a special, specific, graciously idiosyncratic path for each of us. There is a range of timing for each of us, a comeliness peculiar to each of us. Moreover, we are bound to honor, treasure, rejoice in that specialness of faith in ourselves and in others. The diversity we are speaking of is that of life together in Christ, of which we will speak more in the chapter on the mystical body of Christ.

So we are not "losing our faith" if for long, long periods of anger, doubt, confusion we do not trust as we ought. For long, long periods we go into the far countries of our own labyrinthine reasons for not trusting God. But the size and resilience of my own faith and doubt do not begin to amount to the magnitude and resourceful caring of that community to which I belong and of which my baptism is an effective sign. To speak of heroes and heroines of the faith is extremely misleading because it can so easily cause ordinary saints to think they are not Christians because they have — so they would think — "lost their faith."

Love Seeking Understanding

Such confusion about faith — such a propensity to make faith a possession or a way of earning God's favor — usually comes about because faith is considered without sufficient simultaneous attention to the other two cardinal virtues, *hope* and *love* (1 Cor. 13:13). Before going any further, we need to take account of the connections among these virtues.

As regards *hope,* I will be saying something more later about the way the entire presentation of the gospel in the New Testament is concerned with looking forward to the imminent culmination of God's purpose for the world — the "last times."[15] Here I need only point out that a certain perfectionist strain forgets that faith by its very nature is always changing and wavering and

---

15. Contemporary theology is indebted to the persistence with which Jürgen Moltmann pursued the implications of a theology of hope, beginning with his volume of that title: *Theology of Hope* (New York: Harper and Row, 1967).

strengthening as each person grows in different ways in different seasons of life and through wild fluctuations of tragedy and joy. We *live* in hope in the sense that *hope keeps us alive*. Without hope people wither and die. Hope is the envisioning of an alternative to the present and the past and their incorporation, their integration, into new beginnings.[16] Faith is trust that the future belongs to God and therefore there is a place in it for self, for loved ones, for one's enemies, for the environment, for the cosmos: trust that events are leading somewhere and that somewhere is the marriage feast of love and justice.

Of the three most important virtues, *love* is the greatest. Love equals hope-faith squared. What we call hope would be just wishful thinking about vengeance and heavenly gain were it not loving. What we call faith would be just wastrel gullibility were it not continually reshaped by God's love mediated through the forgiven and forgiving community edified and sent by the Holy Spirit.

It is sometimes heard that Protestants believe they are justified by faith whereas Roman Catholics believe they are justified by good works. That is not true. St. Thomas teaches that the faith involved in justification is love-informed faith: faith loaded with love active in good works.[17] While Luther had a quite different understanding of grace than St. Thomas, he knew saving faith is trust busy in the good works Christians are freed by the Word and Spirit to be about. As Luther would say it, we are not justified *by* good works but we are not justified *without* them. Ethics is the coming to action of faith, which is a free gift of the one who is love. A so-called faith, even if it is strong enough to move moun-

16. See the definition of hope in Roy W. Fairchild, *Finding Hope Again* (San Francisco: Harper and Row, 1980).

17. See Aquinas, "On the Exterior Principle of Human Acts, Namely the Grace of God": *Summa Theologica* II, I, Q. 109, Arts. 1-10; Anton Pegis, ed., *Introduction to St. Thomas Aquinas* (New York: Random House, Modern Library, 1948), pp. 650-71.

tains, devoid of love is counterfeit, is no more than the clanging of an empty pan. The whole of 1 Corinthians 13 is about the cost of love freely given and freely received.

The love which informs faith so that it is trust active in good works is ultimately Christ's love. That is one of those pious claims which, though true enough, is used so often that it almost has lost its semantic punch. In fact, however, it is a scandalous claim: a scandalous claim which contains the merriest good news. Our own faith waxes and wanes. Our own faith is sometimes more and sometimes less formed by love. In each condition, the good news is that our wholeness and the wholeness of those around us do not depend on the intensity, continuity, courage of our devotion. Of course, it is *also* our faith and love and hope. But they are faith, hope, and love exactly to the extent that they are responses to the one who engenders, corrects, enflames these responses in us. The one who, in the words of Hebrews, as the "pioneer and perfecter of our faith" enables our sharing in the normative story (Heb. 12:2).

CHAPTER THREE

The Point of Creation

✠   ✠

I believe in God the Father Almighty,
Maker of heaven and earth,
And of all things visible and invisible.

The Divine Chiaroscuro

The first, middle, and last thing to say about creation is that it is good. The goodness of creation is to be confessed at every turn of belief and at every turn of living.

It is not self-evident that creation is good. That creation is good is a calculated confession of faith. The main reason Christians think creation is good is that they claim it is the handiwork of God whom they know through Christ to be good. Creation is good, however, whether or not we recognize that fact, and whether or not we know how we know it.

This confession is easier to make at some times than at others. Often the claim is outlandish in the face of utterly contrary appearances. The church, however, sticks to its conviction that finally, when all is said and done, creation is good and beautiful because it is the result of the intention of God who is good and beautiful.

The contrasting shades, darknesses and lights breaking through, are not incidental to our experience of God's goodness and beauty. God ceaselessly makes his presence known through his natural handiwork. Our egocentric condition distorts our perception. That we fail to see God's self-disclosure does not mean that God ceases to reveal himself through the macrocosm and microcosm he creates and sustains and guides. God's self-accommodation includes the divine chiaroscuro.

Pied Beauty

Glory be to God for dappled things —
    For skies of couple-colour as a brinded cow;
        For rose-moles all in stipple upon trout that swim;
Fresh-firecoal chestnut-falls; finches' wings;
    Landscape plotted and pieced — fold, fallow, and plough;
        And all trades, their gear and tackle and trim.

All things counter, original, spare, strange;
    Whatever is fickle, freckled (who knows how?)
        With swift, slow; sweet, sour; adazzle, dim;
He fathers-forth whose beauty is past change:
        Praise him.[1]

The mottled character of beauty we experience is part of its feasibility, accessibility. It is through appearance to the senses — the "things visible" of the Nicene Creed — that we know goodness; but that reality goes billions of times, light-years' distances, deeper than how we experience it. Today we know that the invisible world extends far, far beyond the visible. Little did the compilers of the creed know of the provision covered by that simple

---

1. Gerard Manley Hopkins, "Pied Beauty," in *The Norton Anthology of Modern Poetry* (New York: Norton, 1973), p. 81.

phrase "and of all things . . . invisible." Visibility refers to that narrow strip on the frequency spectrum that is light. From it we have access to those things that are not directly visible but are put in visible form by technology undreamed of even a few years ago. The things invisible also belong to what is created — indeed, are the dominant background reality, the cosmic sweeps of time and places and energy and many dimensions of deep space.

I have just used a word — "cosmic" — which in common parlance has to do with "creation" and "world." It is a strong word whose laminated meanings merit scrutiny. I am here going to deal only with one of its ancient uses, namely, the claim that there is a correspondence between the large and the small world, between the "macrocosm" and the "microcosm." In this context the former roughly refers to the extended world, the external world, the boundless *magnitude dwelt in*. The latter roughly refers to the personal world, the internal world, the finite *self-indwelling*.[2] That parallel is what is behind those cards available in all the museum shops which show da Vinci's man, arms and legs spread, looking like he is making a snow angel. Beneath it is the ancient dictum, refurbished in the Renaissance, that man is the measure of all things.

Whatever its original uses, this perceived correlation between microcosm and macrocosm underlines five things for us today.

---

2. These terms sometimes have come to be used of astral magnitude and measurement in contrast to subatomic magnitude and measurement. Their use in physics is fascinating and demands further study for the correlations implicit in these comparisons for theological language. Of the burgeoning literature comparing language of theology and physics, see, for examples, John Polkinghorne and Michael Welker, eds., *The End of the World and the Ends of God* (Harrisburg, Pa.: Trinity, 2000); John Polkinghorne, *Quarks, Chaos, and Christianity* (London: Triangle, 1994); and Barbara Brown Taylor, *The Luminous Web: Essays on Science and Religion* (Cambridge, Mass.: Cowley, 2000). I am, however, in this instance using the terms to mean the comparison of the human being and the heavenly spheres.

(1) The observer of creation affects that which is observed. (2) There is a sufficient reliability of physical laws in our part of the universe for us to bet there is a reality to which our language and math correspond, however partially and tentatively. So to speak (that is, if put in speech), the structure of creation is relatively universal. (3) It seems the deeper the observation of the microcosm and the macrocosm, the greater a certain kind of awe in the observer, whether that awe be considered religious or not. (4) Studying the "what" of creation eventually entails some consideration of the "why" of creation. (5) Our expanding knowledge of God's ways with creation bears a distant likeness to what for the moment we take to be the omnidirectional acceleration of the universe. The universe is perfecting, not perfect, and so is our understanding of the correlation between the knowledge of God and the knowledge of selves.

Each of these implications of the macrocosm-microcosm tie needs explication, which I am undertaking elsewhere. Here I want to begin with "so to speak" — the nature of the language the creed uses about creation.

What "Father," "Creator," and "Almighty" Say and Do Not Say

"Creation," "creature," "world," "universe," "creator," "time," "goal," "beginning," "we" — these basic terms, and others like them, already reflect major assumptions about the very questions we are asking. Take "to create." The verb is used to cover thousands of kinds of events (another loaded term), but they all apparently have this in common: someone does something to existing material to bring about a new thing even though it may be a copy of something on hand before. Some kind of motion (another loaded term) with some kind of material results (ditto) in something else. We talk and think this way because we do not have anything else to compare "to create" to. When we think about "the purpose" or think about "where things come from," we are thinking and speaking comparatively. Language works by analogies — by people making the same comparisons enough of the time so they have a workable idea of what another person means by this or that expressed image. Analogies — working comparisons — point to ways two things are alike and to ways two things are not the same. When we say that God is creator and that God is father and that God is almighty, we are using analogies, that is, comparison that says both what God is like and what God is not.

To say something by analogy is not to say it less truly than if we were to speak and think literally. When it comes to the most important realities, we seem most to rely on using the richest analogies possible. The use of apt analogies is, when it comes to matters of ultimate concern and ultimate delight, the way we can be the most accurate and powerful and clear. To compare God's creating to that of a parent says far more and says it more accurately than literalist reductions. Literalist reductions are only expressions using the narrowest band of analogies; analogies in some form or another are inevitable in human thought and speech. "She helped me pick up the pieces" says the reality more than "She was an integrating influence in my life." By the same token, though, when "picking up the pieces" becomes overused, "integration" may be the strongest wording. "When I got through customs, he caught me in one of his bear hugs" says the reality more accurately than "He greeted me warmly." By the same token, though, when "bear hug" becomes trite — loses its image-making power through overuse — then the understated "greeted me warmly" may be the most moving poetry. In that case "warmly" is the operative analogy! So it is with expressions like "crystal clear," eyes like "deep wells," "quivers" full of children, someone being "the cornerstone," a person being "covered by the garment of Christ's righteousness," "on earth as it is in heaven." And so on.

So when we say "I believe in God the Father Almighty, Maker . . . ," the main thing by far that we are doing is confessing our trust in God to be like a loving parent on whom we can rely no matter when, no matter where, no matter what. It is undeniable, I think, that for far too long the language about God as Father diminished the range of meaning that goes with thinking and speaking of God as loving parent.[3] In cultures or family units where fatherhood is experienced as arbitrary, oppressive, and abusive, calling God that kind of father is blasphemous: it says God is the opposite of a loving parent. Just substituting the title "Mother" may supply a certain welcome relief for those who have had better luck with mothers than with fathers; but the abuse of power is not gender-specific to men, any more than strong nurturing is gender-specific to women.

The scandal is that we dare think of God in personal terms at all, that we dare compare God either to a father or to a mother. Some religions avoid that imagery altogether, or do not think there is purposeful care for creation. That dismissal of personal imagery for a "Supreme Being" has much to commend itself, especially because it takes away any basis for blaming a god for this or that eruption of what we mortals would otherwise consider to be evil. However, the biblical view of God, Old and New Testament, makes the unrelenting claim that God is personal, and is personal in an ultimately benevolent, caring, strategic way. That is why the Bible repeatedly proclaims God to be especially watchful for those people in society that are oppressed.

We have seen how central to the biblical view of God is the

3. See Elizabeth A. Johnson, "The Incomprehensibility of God and the Image of God Male and Female," *Theological Studies* 45, no. 3 (September 1984): 441-80, and Elizabeth A. Johnson, *She Who Is* (New York: Crossroad, 1992).

constellation of events we know as the exodus. Central to the exodus is the fact that God is personal in that he *hears* the cry of his people and *does* something about their plight. Time and time again the prophets teach that God has a predilection for those who have none to speak for them, none to execute justice on their behalf, none to turn to for relief from their poverty and sickness, none to liberate them. In our days, that applies to racial injustice, to the plight of those decimated by rampant HIV, to the children who are appallingly exploited, to those trapped in refugee camps, to the starving, to all those whose care is the Messiah's signature. (See the whole of Luke 4:1-30.) John the Baptizer asks from prison, "Are you he who is to come?" and Christ's reply is, "Go and tell John what you have seen and heard: the blind receive their sight, the lame walk, lepers are cleansed, and the deaf hear, the dead are raised up, the poor have good news preached to them. And blessed is he who takes no offense at me" (Luke 7:18-23). *Not* incidentally, the penultimate clause does not mean that the poor get preaching instead of justice. It means that the poor hear the good news that the Day of the Lord is at hand, the time when the conditions described in the Magnificat will happen — a radical reversal, utter upheaval, of power and privilege.

James Cone rightly calls the true God the God of the oppressed.[4] God is personal in hearing and doing — and in holding to account those who think they worship rightly but sell the poor for a pair of shoes, who despise the widows and orphans. God's being personal defines what ultimately is full personhood. Doing so — thinking and speaking of God as parent — commits us to the kind and magnitude of compassionate, wise, effective care that human parents aspire to but at best only approximate. Yet we

---

4. James H. Cone, *God of the Oppressed* (New York: Seabury Press, 1974). See also Harold A. Carter, *The Prayer Tradition of Black People* (Valley Forge, Pa.: Judson, 1976).

are, for all that inadequacy and perilous discourse, taught by Christ to pray, "Our Father who is in heaven. . . ." That means, among other things, that the Father who is in heaven is not made in the image of earthly parents, and that earthly parents are to care for others as does God who gives bread enough for each day. More is going on with this part of the creed, but that is the central thing, especially when we remember the distinction between *believing that* and *believing in*. We say we *believe in* because we are confessing, and pledging ourselves to, a personal trust in God who is both behind everything good and is like a loving parent. Of course, we *believe that* to be the case, but the trusting quality of the affirmation is the main point.

What we know as love here and now is derivative of God's *being love* eternally. Getting this as straight as possible will give us a clue about two things the creed is *not* saying about creation and the Creator.

First, it is *not* saying that only God the Father is the Creator. The doctrine of the Trinity is not that the "Father" is the "God" who has two assistants, the "Son" and the "Spirit." That was a fight the church had to engage in: to insist that by God we mean the Holy Trinity, and so the Son and the Spirit no less than the Father are united to be the eternal love who is God. The creed, further on, says Jesus Christ is the enfleshed Eternal Son "by whom all things were made," and it goes on to call the Holy Spirit the "Lord and giver of life." It is the Holy Triune who is love and who loves creation into existence. Yes, this activity is more assigned in our thought and language to this way of God's being God, but technically it is the whole unity — the Holy Triune — who is Creator, Redeemer, and Sanctifier.

Second, the creed is *not* saying that God is *all-doing* when it says he is *almighty*. The point of creation is not just that God have another to receive his love, but also that the creature have the joy of responding to that love with love. A loving response is not a

44

compelled, mechanical response: it entails free choice of what to do and think and feel with the resources, potential, we are given. The capacity is indeed given, and the continual motion of love by God toward us is continually prompting us. That is what grace is: the gift of God's presence to evoke reciprocal love. Being created in the image of God includes having the capacity to respond in this or that way, including ways which go contrary to the love of God, of others, and of self. There is human accountability, and there is weight to human action. Human creativity and human destructiveness have an effect on the unfolding dynamic of the creation. In fact, as is evident more and more with the explosion of technology, the boundaries between human activity and other creaturely activity are less and less clear. Just take what humans are able to do with establishing genomes and with cloning, activity as awesome in its capacity for good or for evil as the unleashing of atomic power. God is powerful enough to limit God's self to make room for human activity, either to reject or to embrace God's loving purposes.[5]

God being God, however, means that ultimately God will have his benevolent way. Ultimately grace, not destruction, is sovereign. In the meantime, if we are to judge from the diversity of biblical accounts, we surmise that by perseverance, patient and relentless, God is seeking to be understood as love and responded to as love. God's parental inclusive power means that God must, like any parent, time after time not intervene and so see beloved children go their ways and learn hard lessons from those ways. Yet sometimes parental love means unmistakable intervention, as in the accounts of freeing the slaves in Egypt. Pa-

---

5. See William C. Placher, *Narratives of a Vulnerable God: Christ, Theology, and Scripture* (Louisville: Westminster John Knox, 1994); William C. Placher, "The Vulnerability of God," in *Toward the Future of Reformed Theology*, ed. D. Willis and M. Welker (Grand Rapids: Eerdmans, 1999). Cf. also David Willis, *Notes on the Holiness of God* (Grand Rapids: Eerdmans, 2002).

rental love means that one is exposed to rejection and to the agony of not being able, time and again, to do for the children what they must do for themselves if they are to grow into their own maturity. That comes with the territory of love freely given and freely returned. Or not returned. The true God has the power to suffer rejection without repaying in kind, the power to become human, the power to become flesh and dwell among us full of grace and truth.[6] It is this specific power that is especially confessed when we say and sing that we believe in God the almighty parent who stands behind, and has an ultimately sovereign purpose for, the creation loved into existence and continually guided and upheld by that love.

Covenant and Creation in That Order

That God is love should jump out at us as a scandalous claim in the face of the cruelty, tragedy, and seemingly capricious things that happen all the time to people. Why not confess, instead, that there is no apparent rhyme or reason to this or that event? Surely that is what almost everyone sooner or later would honestly believe to be the case — either that, or believe that sometimes God (if there is such a reality) is a tormenting power, or that at best God seems just a well-intentioned but impotent and bumbling artificer. The scandal is the claim that God is ultimately trustworthily benevolent and has a purpose that we often as not cannot discern but must trust is at work. That scandal is of such a magnitude that it dwarfs, by comparison, unedifying squabbles over the exact number of days and the literal meaning of days and the first-week progression and similar details of ancient Middle East cosmologies. In fact, precisely because the Genesis sagas are part

6. See Karl Barth, *The Humanity of God* (Richmond, Va.: John Knox, 1960).

of the written form of the Word of God, we learn from them far more than ancient Middle East cosmology.[7]

So what makes this part of the creed *informed trust* rather than just an antiquarian leftover or, worse, blindered wishful thinking? It is the covenant. More accurately, it is Israel's experience of God's covenantal fidelity. By adopting and adapting the creation sagas behind the Genesis accounts, Israel is identifying the Creator with the gracious Covenant Initiator. In this sense the covenant is the presupposition of creation, just as — we shall see later — the triumph of the good news is the presupposition of true repentance. The creation sagas, as adopted and adapted by Israel and considered to be part of Israel's normative writings, are part of Israel's proclamatory remembering: we know from God's covenanting benevolence that God is one and that all creation belongs to him and that he brought it into existence for his purposes.

Knowledge of the covenant is what makes the creed on this point an article of *informed* trust. This is true of the history of God's covenanting in the Old Testament, but even more so in the New: "This cup is the new covenant in my blood" (1 Cor. 11:25; cf. Matt. 26:28; Mark 14:24; and with reference to the cup and bread, Luke 22:14-23). What is at stake in the act of creating in the first place (actually, to make the first place) is more fully disclosed in what believers experience as "being made new" and being "new creatures." It is from its restoration that believers — so they claim — realize more fully than ever before what it means to be created in the image of God.[8] It is in the process of maturing in love that

7. On the creation sagas, see Bernhard W. Anderson, *Creation versus Chaos* (New York: Association, 1967). The classic explication of the relation between covenant and creation remains Karl Barth, *Church Dogmatics* I/1–IV/1 (Edinburgh: T. & T. Clark, 1936-69), III/1, par. 41.

8. See Calvin on the image of God being known from its restoration: *Institutes of the Christian Religion,* ed. J. T. McNeill, trans. F. L. Battles, 2 vols. (Philadelphia: Westminster, 1960), 1.15.4, pp. 189-90.

they more and more realize what they were created to become. As they mature in this freedom, they more and more realize that they and others, also created in the image of God, have never lost that identity, no matter how tragically they have practiced its grievous distortion.

That is what sin is, the willful distortion of the image of God into which the human community was created. That image is everything that makes up the capacity to love, the capacity for joyful wholeness in relation. Love is what we came into existence for in the first place. That, ultimately, is the point of it all, and ultimately the only point. What the loving God creates is meant for love. Creation comes about because God wills into existence another with whom to share his love. We know this preeminently from the lengths to which this loving God goes — into the far country — to overcome those things that alienate us from others, from self, and from God.

The words I am using here — "love," "purpose," "joy," "wholeness" — are overworked to such an extent that we hear them without their bite. They are like bland organ stops with no chiff. They are, however, the only words we have without introducing even more bland jargon. In any event, here is an essential part of the creedal conviction that probably needs to be sung so that its importance is felt at the deepest level of our hearts and minds: God's being love is what is behind creation. Creation comes about and continues — nanosecond by nanosecond, billion years by billion years, quantum leap by quantum leap, multidimension by multidimension, energy burst by energy burst, expansion by expansion — because of God's being love prior to there coming into existence anything that has ever come into existence.

Isn't this doxological language, imprecise exclamation? Of course it is — and therefore the language most congruent for referring to the Subject who goes beyond all human thought, imagination, speech, including mathematical formulae which are as detailed a way of responding to physical reality as any media we have. When I say "the being of God," I mean God's being eternally relation, what the church adoringly sings of as "the Holy Trinity." "Oh," we may say, "but I've never been able to understand the Trinity." Welcome to the club! Rather, welcome to the communion of saints! Mystery in this context does not refer to what we do not know, or to what is discovered step-by-step in a plot of a mystery novel, or to riddle, or to enigma. Mystery refers to that which is hidden in its very disclosure: it is revealed to be by its very nature also hidden. This mystery is revealed and proclaimed hiddenness.

For Jonathan Edwards the unfolding purposes of God are made explicit and actual in Christ's desire to communicate his happiness *and* in Christ's desire to be known by the society thereby made to share Christ's happiness. The whole of creation comes about because of the desire of God to communicate himself to another. We find that in Edwards's *Miscellanies* and in his *End for Which the World Was Created:* "The Son is the adequate communication of the Father's goodness, is an express and complete image of him. But yet the Son has also an inclination to communicate himself, in an image of his person that may partake of his happiness: and this was the end of the creation, even the communication of the happiness of the Son of God: and this was the only motive hereto, even the Son's inclination to this. . . . And man, the consciousness or perception of the creation, is the immediate subject of this" (*Miscellanies* 104).[9]

The communication of the divine happiness is the end for

9. See Louis Mitchell, *Jonathan Edwards on the Experience of Beauty* (Princeton: Princeton Theological Seminary, 2003). For a fuller treatment of Edwards's doctrine of creation and his Christology, see Sang Hung Lee, *The Philosophical Theology of Jonathan Edwards* (Princeton: Princeton University Press, 1988), and Anri Morimoto, *Jonathan Edwards and the Catholic Vision of Salvation* (University Park: Pennsylvania State University Press, 1995).

which God created the world. That conviction has dropped from the ken of the conscientious, earnest, compacted religion that settles for a kind of low-key misery as if pain in itself were more virtuous than joy. Probably this morbid suspicion of happiness is a protective device by which we guard ourselves from loss. Probably it is distrust that comes from the superstition that those whom the gods destroy they first make happy. Then there is the confusion of happiness with having a happy day enjoined upon the unwary by grinning bumper stickers.

The bold alternative to these aberrations is to see that informed trust also often breaks forth in joyful abandon. The quality of thanksgiving is not restrained. At least according to biblical poetic, the hills and trees laugh and clap their hands and make a joyful noise at God's doing. Calvin, contrary to the expectations of those who paint him and the Calvinists with the same brush, is lucid on this point. God could just as well have created the world for its usefulness, but he created it also for its delight. God could have given us food just to keep our bodies going, but he made the food to be a source of joy.[10] The same with flowers and the other gracious provisions of a loving parent. It is delicious to be caught up in God's unstinting love and to be lavish in our love of what God has created.

We have but the tiniest inkling of the magnitude and richness of God's love, much less of what it means to say that God is love prior to all creation and brought into existence the energy, space, time — everything inconceivable out of which original and continuing creation *is*. Yet there is an inkling, a poetic parlance, a distant analogy for God's loving another into existence: the dynamics of growth in love between two persons. It is love of the kind that treats the other as a subject of reciprocal delight and not as an

---

10. For Calvin's teaching that God created for our delight, not just for our use, see *Institutes* 3.10.2; McNeill ed., pp. 720-21.

object of calculating use. For in a relationship of mutual edification, encouragement, and delight, the more one knows the other
the more one realizes the depth of the other. In that relationship
we do not "master" the other, get the other "down pat." Rather
we go from one startling new discovery of unimagined dimensions to the next. The more you know about the other person, the
more you are in wonderment at the mystery of the other's being.

That also applies to the growing self-knowledge in this kind
of relationship. Dimensions of oneself are discovered in this process in which *hiddenness is part of what is revealed.* That is why we
totally misunderstand the nature of the creed if we think it is a
means of explaining away the mystery. In fact, it is just the opposite: the creed serves to locate, identify, point as accurately as possible to the mystery of God's love toward us and God's being eternally love prior to all things. God as love is prior to priority, since
God as love is before time and space and energy. God does *have*
love, of course; but it is truer to say that God *is* love.

Cocreator in the Creator's Image

Above we referred to God creating humans in the divine image.
There we said the image of God into which we are created — the
image toward which we were created[11] — is above all characterized by love. Moreover, that love is understood as being open for
other persons and for delighting in other parts of creation. This

---

11. Irenaeus was right: God created Adam and Eve with all their potentials
but not perfect. They were created to grow forward to the fulfillment of their
humanity in Christ. Eden was not a perfect place, but the place where the journey toward wholeness began. Sin harms that capacity to grow whole, harms the
capacity to mature. Grace restores that capacity. See Gustaf Wingren, *Man and
the Incarnation: A Study of the Biblical Theology of Irenaeus* (Philadelphia:
Muhlenberg, 1959).

love delights in the good of another over one's own good and finds one's own delight in the other. That capacity for another is, paradoxically, the way we find our own identity.

Now we have to say something more about the practice of that image. I mean the practicalities by which we struggle to live humanely — not angelically nor brutishly, but humanely.

Growth in the image is costly. This particular growth is grace, but not cheap grace.[12] We are continually tested, and through that testing we grow. That is our share in the ongoing creation. Minuscule though our part in continuing creation may be, that growth is still part of the outward and forward movement of all creation. Our growth in testing is in part what it means to be a creature, not the Creator, just as we are called to be a disciple, not the Savior. Our part in the growth of creation is our taking the times and spaces and energy given us and making the greater good with them — just as we saw earlier that genuine spirituality is the materiality of working with the wild stones of the abbey.

There are no shortcuts, no end arounds which bypass the ambiguities, pains, joys, mixed terrain common to all human life. Our being created in the image of God means that we are cocreators not in escaping the lot of other humans, but in the practice of love in the quandaries of successive tests. Jacob wrestles to become Israel (Gen. 32:22-32). Thereafter he limps — as a sign of his wholeness. So with all God's people. It is in the struggle that the image of God is tested and matured. The passion for some sense to our lives and to the lives of others — the passion for some sense of how this or that tragedy or triumph fits into the whole — is in large measure what it means for humans to be cocreators created in the image of the singular Creator. "What is

12. On the distinction between costly (true) grace and cheap (false) grace, see Dietrich Bonhoeffer, *The Cost of Discipleship* (New York: Macmillan, 1965), chap. 1, "Grace and Discipleship," pp. 45-114.

the point of it all?" is a question wrung out of people sooner or later, sometimes as an outward expression, sometimes as an inward gnawing. The question, depending on the inflection, can be an expression of wonder, say, at the magnitude and brilliance of the luminaries of our galaxy, or it can be a cry of desperate grief in the face, say, of relentless loss. Either way, the question is about purpose — or lack thereof.

One of the great ironies of the human psyche is that it is because of the very presence of hope for goodness and beauty — because of the guess that the world and our lives should make sense — that *we are a questioning species.* We measure conditions and experiences by some inherent alternative — some culturally mediated memory, as it were. Perhaps we are restless with archetypal hopes. Some standard of goodness and beauty is supposed when we raise the question why this or that condition and not something more. When Socrates said that the unexamined life is not worth living, he did not know how far that observation went. The more human a life, the more questioning it is. There is a correlation between maturing as a human and wanting to get at the freeing truth. There is no maturation, no development of the person, without it. Dumb acquiescence is not what we were created for. Humans are created questing, wondering. That questing may be almost drummed out of them. It may be almost smothered by the weight of injustice, apathy, and loss. However, part of what it means to be created in the image of God is to look for, to test, to be curious about, to chew on, to ponder. Human asking is part of the goodness of creation, and woe to us if we smother the child-like (not childish) drive to ask why.

The image of God into which we are created is above all the capacity for life-enhancing relation with others, with God, and with those parts of the universe within our purview. That being in right relationship is usually spoken of, in the Christian tradition at least, in terms of proportionality, aptness, congruence. We are who we are because of the fittingness of our response to who God is toward us. "I am the LORD your God, who . . . You shall . . ." (Deut. 5:6ff.; Exod. 20:2ff.). Here I need only add that this being in right relationship includes the integration of the various things — ideas, emotions, economic condition, physical health, hunger for righteousness, delights, artistic drives, and so on — which make up who we are intended to become.

The word for the condition to which we are being delivered is one I have already used: "integrity." Integrity is wholeness, unsplinteredness, unfragmentedness. We are invoking this imagery when we say so-and-so or such and such "rings true." Wholeness in this sense is held-togetherness: as crystal or a forged bell is a "resounding" holding together of things in tension. Tension is not incidental to integration, for the tensile strength of something is the way its component particles cohere, are congruent. The tensioned parts "fit." They belong together to make up a whole, and are most themselves in that tensioned co-belonging. Integrity is being integrated! Integrity in this sense is a progressing condition, not a fixed state.

The ancients spoke of the body, soul, and mind as a kind of triad which stood for the whole person — what, incidentally, the "heart" stood for prior to this popularity of the body-soul-mind triad. The image of God into which we are created is not one of these at the expense of the others. Sickness unto death, quite literally when we consider psychosomatic illness, comes with attending to one or two of these dimensions while denigrating or ignoring the other(s). According to Gregory of Nazianzus (as we shall see in the next chapter), the incarnation means that the Eternal Word took up the whole human condition, mind, body, and soul.[13] The mind, the body, the soul are all healed by God's inter-

<hr />

13. Gregory Nazianzus, Epistle 101, To Cledonius against Apollinaris, in E. R. Hardy, ed., *Christology of the Later Fathers* (Philadelphia: Westminster, 1954),

vening love. Of the three, the body has been the most poorly treated in a large section of Christianity, just as it has in other religions. It is often dealt with by religions only as a hot spot of trouble, rather than primarily as a good dimension of human wholeness, created as much for delight as for utility.

The body as much as the mind and the soul is precious to God. Often the soul gets a disproportionate amount of attention in many religions. In popular parlance, it is almost as if religion by definition were that which deals with the soul. We often hear about "the journey of the soul," but we hear little about "the journey of the body" or "the journey of the mind." Evangelism was widely considered a matter of saving souls. Such relative denigration of the body needs correction. The materiality of the creed will help make that correction. The implications of treating the body as equally good because it is the creation of the good God are far-reaching. We turn to some of those implications now.

The Glory of Taking Time to Create out of Nothing

Above we considered the belief that the point of creation is to share the divine happiness. God creates as much for our delight as for our use. We considered, next, the belief that the image of God is a matter of the proportionality of the whole person — what body, soul, and mind stand for. Putting these beliefs together, we see that the practice of being created in the image of God is to de-

---

pp. 218-20. Here again is the catholic affirmation of the incarnation expressed in terms of the assumption of human nature by the Eternal Word. Note that Brunner chose Luther's dictum on this ("Nostra assumsit, ut conferret nobis sua") as one of the two banner texts at the front of *The Mediator* (Philadelphia: Westminster, 1947). The other text Brunner chose for this prominence was that of Irenaeus: "Jesus Christ, in His infinite love, has become what we are, in order that He may make us entirely what He is."

light in the right relatedness of body, soul, and mind. There seem to be times and branches of Christianity that are more attentive to one dimension of the human self than to another.

It seems that taking sane delight in the body has been the most difficult to get straight. The factors behind that all-too-frequent denigration of the body are complex and numerous. Sometimes the denigration comes from a fear of not being able to be in control of bodily deliciousness. That is, downplaying the body is a kind of protection against the overwhelming distraction of creaturely beauty. Sometimes, though, the reason is quite the opposite. The body is suspect not because it is so dangerously beautiful, but because it is considered inherently less good than the mind and surely less good than the soul. The idea here is that the more physical, material, worldly, bodily a thing, the less good it is. Part of creation is good and part of creation is bad, and the body mainly is on the side of the bad. Oh — so this line of thinking goes — the body may be good insofar as it is useful, but to delight in it is to enjoy what ought to be valued only for its usefulness. This dualism is an ever present danger, the more so because of its pervasive subtlety. It crops up in each of us whenever we succumb to the temptation to punish the body for its bodilyness — or whenever we punish the mind and the psyche for paying attention to the somatic dimension of humanness.

As with most tenacious views, there are compelling psychological reasons for dualism's many forms and longevity. For example, it would be a comfort to some to think this world is just a vale of tears through which the soul passes as little contaminated by it as possible. Again, it would be a comfort to some to think of one's sickly, pain-ridden, deformed, aging body as a shell indwelt by a noble, immortal soul. Dualism provides some with a satisfying rebellion against the sure lesson of finitude that the corruptible body makes. Back of these forms of dualism are the ideas that changelessness and goodness are equivalent, and that the soul is of a higher goodness because (supposedly) it is less subject to change than the body. Death, accordingly, is a blessed release of the soul to heaven, a realm of perfection in contrast to this troubled, loss-filled world. What is hoped for, to draw on the language of physics, is a return to perfect symmetry and the reversal of differentiation, a folding back up of what has unfolded. Dualism in its several forms holds that matter is opposed to spirit, body is opposed to soul, light is opposed to darkness, and that wholeness for the human is escape from the body and return — or advance — to the realm of pure spirit. In popular terms: the less body, the better off you are.

Instead of this dualism, the church believes in the incarnation and in the resurrection of the body. She also believes that God created all things visible and invisible "out of nothing," and did so "in the beginning."

There is no way, however, of denying the church's frequent complicity in some forms of dualism. Christianity in some of its forms has been one of the main conveyors of some forms of dualism — and still is. The great Augustine was deeply influenced by Neoplatonism, which he embraced as alternative to a much cruder dualism. Nonetheless, when it came to describing evil, Augustine argued that evil is not one of two equal but opposing forces of the universe, good being the other. He defined evil derivatively: evil is the privation of good, not the other way round.[14] In the formula "creation out of nothing," "nothing" is not a negative something alongside God that God takes and does the best he can with. God is good, so what he creates is good — all of it. Evil, the privation of good, is a diminution of creation, is a threatened slipping back into chaos. It may be that Augustine did not go far enough by not rejecting a final dualism implied in the eternal sep-

14. For Augustine's treatment of *creatio ex nihilo* and evil as *privatio boni,* see Peter Brown, *Augustine of Hippo* (Berkeley: University of California Press, 1969).

aration of some who are going to heaven and some who are going to hell. Still, he saw that the doctrine of creation out of nothing preserved the essential truth that insofar as something is (not just *exists* but *is* — has *being*), it is good. It is good because it is created by God who is good, by God who looks on his handiwork and sees that it is good.

Today the "in the beginning" of creation seems less and less like a mythic expression. The primitive imagery has, as it were, a new life when we go back further in time and thus in distance to the start of the universe. I am not saying that the editors of Genesis and the astrophysicists are saying the same thing, much less that the findings of any physics can be used to bolster any ancient cosmology. What I am saying, however, is that the biblical editors and the astrophysicists have in common at least (maybe more, but at least these) three things. First, they share an awed not-knowing — an awed agnosticism — about what is prior to and beyond the act of creation. Second, they share a curiosity-driven need to inquire into and speak of the ultimate form of matter. Third, they both must speak of these matters in their respective linguistic currencies, which are richly analogical. I think it much a matter of semantics whether one consider mathematical formulae to be linguistic actions. But at least it is true that when they choose to speak in the vulgar tongue — to put their statements into words — both resort to their own forms of *poesis*. Just as there is a *theopoesis*,[15] there is an *astropoesis*.[16] Take the following sentence, in which the single quotation marks are guards against literalism. *"A 'point' of 'energy' 'was' all there 'was' 'before' and 'beyond' 'time' and 'space' 'were.'"* Because we are accustomed to using language

15. Cf. Amos Wilder, *Theopoetic* (Philadelphia: Fortress, 1976).

16. While I am loath to create terms unnecessarily, I think it arguable — and I am presently engaged in a project so to argue — that *astropoesis* is a correlate of *theopoesis,* in the sense that *poesis* in both cases is a special kind of analogical discourse particularly appropriate to their respective subjects.

this way, we know that the guards are implied and we say simply that before the start of creation there was an unimaginable, dimensionless, atemporal point of energy. The words are truthful to the extent that they are nonliteral pointers to dimensions of para-verbal reality. *Poesis,* whether discoursing about the ultimate Subject or his creation, is a way of pointing accurately to realms of reality which transcend the poverty of literalism.

CHAPTER FOUR

The Person of Christ

✠   ✠

We believe in one Lord, Jesus Christ, the only Son of God, eternally begotten of the Father, God from God, Light from Light, true God from true God, begotten not made, of one Being with the Father. Through him all things were made. For us and our salvation he came down from heaven: by the power of the Holy Spirit he became incarnate from the Virgin Mary, and was made man. For our sake he was crucified under Pontius Pilate; he suffered death and was buried. On the third day . . .

Christ Clothed with His Benefits

The affective tradition in Christology observed that to know Christ is to enjoy his benefits. Knowing what those benefits are is not enough. We do not really understand what those benefits are until we experience them for ourselves, as they apply to us. They are such that the experience we have of them is primarily that of enjoyment. Those benefits are the fruits of who Jesus Christ is and what he does.

It is impossible to think of Jesus Christ apart from his work. The same is true of trying to conceive of his works apart from his personal identity.[1] His name says the two sides of the same reality: "Jesus Christ" means that Jesus comes doing what the prophets said the Messiah ("Christ") would be doing, and the given name means that the unlikely one ushering in the kingdom of God is Mary's boy Jesus. When we treat the person of Christ (in this chapter), we will deal primarily with *the being of the Mediator,* and when we treat the work of Christ (in the next chapter), we will deal primarily with *the doing of the Mediator.*

That does not mean that his works exhaustively define him, nor that his person is all we have of him. It means that by his inseparable action and person he is *the Mediator of creation* and the *Mediator of salvation.*[2] That is, the one by whom all things were created is the same one in whom all things are given their place in the divine happiness for which the world was created. "Sin" is the word we use for the radical departure from that benevolent intention, and "salvation" is the word we use for the overcoming of sin. Sin is fully identifiable only in relation to the goodness that overcomes it. Sin is the manifold choice to live ignoring the sovereign love that is behind all. Salvation is the restoration of original integrity *plus.* Salvation is the restoration of right relation to God, to others, and to self — *plus* the joy of knowing the depths to which God goes in his movement into our condition and the heights of blessedness to which he raises us in his victory.

Just as it is impossible to conceive of Christ's person apart from his works, it is impossible to conceive of Christ apart from those he has united to himself by the bond of the Holy Spirit.

1. Hans W. Frei, *The Identity of Jesus Christ: The Hermeneutical Bases of Dogmatic Theology* (Philadelphia: Fortress, 1975).

2. For an eminently balanced, informed, and clear doctrine of the person and mission of Jesus, see William C. Placher's *Jesus the Savior: The Meaning of Jesus Christ for Christian Faith* (Louisville: Westminster John Knox, 2001). See also Leanne Van Dyk, *Believing in Jesus Christ* (Louisville: Geneva Press, 2002).

Christ is *the Mediator of* creation and redemption, but Christ is thereby also *the Mediator mediated.* I mean by that two things.

First, I mean that Christ is the content, the identifying reality, of the sovereign love that is behind creation and salvation. He is not only the way of mediation. He is the goal of that mediation. Here the universal claims are unavoidable: God was in Christ reconciling *the world* to himself, and in him will *all things* be recapitulated.

Second, I mean that Christ's mediation has a history to it. The creating and healing knowledge of his person and work is mediated through the people he joins to himself. We have only mediated, not immediate, access to Jesus Christ. The biblical Jesus is the one proclaimed to be the Christ, a composite of the presentations of him evoked by his reality among those who proclaim his identity. Their interpretations are of one whose person and work evoke amazed response. He is not reducible to their presentations, any more than a historical event can be reduced to its interpretation. To use Tillich's terminology, the happening is what gets interpreted to constitute historical event. The event of Jesus Christ, his person and work, includes the effect on those who retell it, who actively re-present his creating and saving deeds.

She Named Him King Jesus

The event is painted often: two women reaching out to embrace each other. They are great with Israel's future. Mary carries her baby Jesus, Elizabeth carries John, to be called the Baptizer. Elizabeth's face shows the jump in her womb. According to Luke's Gospel, even in the womb John was welcoming the one he later proclaimed, at mortal price to himself, to be the anointed one whom faithful Israel awaited.

As the birth narratives go on, Luke makes it clear that the whole of creation is alerted to the birth of this baby. That is what the story of the star and the displaced sages is all about. So also the words of Simeon later in the temple:

> Lord, now lettest thou thy servant depart in peace,
> according to thy word;
> for mine eyes have seen thy salvation
> which thou hast prepared in the presence of all peoples,
> a light for revelation to the Gentiles,
> and for glory to thy people Israel. (Luke 2:29-32)

This one born in the stable, attended by shepherds and their ilk, and later cradled in Simeon's arms is the light of all the nations. *O magnum mysterium!*

As Luke presents the case, the imperial census had a point beyond counting people. It is the way the Messiah comes to be born in the city of David as prophesied.[3] The point of the story is that the baby Jesus is not just the Messiah and true King of Israel (as Herod feared in Matthew's account). He is the Lord, the key to understanding and bringing about God's universal purposes. By the time Luke's Gospel was told, written, and edited, the good news was already being proclaimed everywhere by the chosen apostles: Jesus of Nazareth has been vindicated as the longed-for Jewish Christ and the Lord of the whole inhabited earth. The book of Acts and the Gospel according to Luke were written primarily by the same author to proclaim the same reality for Jews and Gentiles, the same creed *in nuce:* "Jesus, Christ, Lord."

I have used the terms "Old Testament" and "New Testament." Those terms, as we have noted, are controversial. Their use is already a confession about the continuity and discontinuity

---

3. Matthew sees it differently. He has no need to invoke the census because he has Jesus born in Bethlehem and Mary and Joseph moving to Nazareth after their return from exile in Egypt.

of Israel's and the church's experience of God's covenanting fidelity. The relation between the two Testaments, however, is not that one deals with creation and the other does not, or that one deals with redemption and the other does not. Rather, in sticking with the writings of God's people up to the time of Jesus' coming as the Christ, the church is betting on the fact that both forms of God's people worship the same God. Both Testaments deal with creation and redemption. The fulfillment of the purposes of creation entails overcoming that which hinders God's benevolent purposes; and redemption entails a new creation as the glorious recapitulation of the old. It is God's ceaseless identity and providential strategy that determine the continuity and discontinuity of Old and New Testaments. "For what we preach is not ourselves, but Jesus Christ as Lord, with ourselves as your servants for Jesus' sake. For it is the God who said, 'Let light shine out of darkness,' who has shone in our hearts to give the light of the knowledge of the glory of God in the face of Christ" (2 Cor. 4:5-6).

It is in the identity of the Christ that redemption is seen to be the restoration of the ability to mature into the humans God intended for us to become, *and* it is in the identity of Christ that creation is seen to be setting in motion that sovereign love which is capable of becoming fully human. Creation and redemption are defined in terms of each other, because the one who redeems is the same one by whom all things were made. There is no analogy for that uniqueness, even though the language we use to point to it is of course analogical. The incarnation of the Eternal Word by whom all things are made is not one in a series. The Eternal does not become human every day, though the ripple effect of that uniqueness happens all the time in ways we need to be alerted to and thankful for.

There is a loose popular spirituality that speaks easily of this or that "incarnating" itself. That slippery language is an example of how the unique incarnation is used as an analogy for the ongoing presence and work of the Holy Spirit in calling and edifying men and women in their co-membership in the body of Christ. I will take up the legitimacy of these strong claims in the following chapters on what the creed says about the Holy Spirit and the church. Here I just want to make it as clear as possible that the fundamental disclosed mystery of the Christian faith is the incarnation of the Eternal Word. The incarnation is the begetting in time and place — the scandalously particular time and space of Mary — of the Word eternally begotten.

This mystery is a matter of the most radical simplicity. The incarnation is not radically simple because it is "understandable" — which it is not. The incarnation is the radical simplicity of the uniqueness of God living humanly: fully God, fully human, one person. There were, and are, all sorts of ways of slipping off this radical healing uniqueness. The church — as we saw in chapter 1 — had to expand the creed to deal with these efforts which sought in this or that alternative formulation to slip off the scandalous, healing particularity of Jesus Christ being really God really living humanly as really a person.

We will briefly remind ourselves of these major temptations, which would have minimized the mystery's boundless depth, would have sought to make the salvific mystery more manageable for human understanding and accessible logic.

The Twice Begetting of the Eternal Word

Just as we saw with the Genesis descriptions of creation, so too with the prologue of the Gospel according to John. They are both centrally interested in dealing with the point of it all. What, if anything or anyone, can make at least some sense of what is going on? What, if anything, can people look forward to? John's Gospel ups the ante.

In the beginning was the Word, and the Word was with God, and the Word was God. He was in the beginning with God; all things were made through him, and without him was not anything made that was made. In him was life, and the life was the light of men. The light shines in the darkness, and the darkness has not overcome it. There was a man sent from God, whose name was John. He came for testimony, to bear witness to the light, that all might believe through him. He was not the light, but came to bear witness to the light. . . . And the Word became flesh and dwelt among us, full of grace and truth; we have beheld his glory, glory as of the only Son from the Father. (John 1:1-8, 14)

The prologue dares address the *question about what is reasonably to be hoped* in terms of *who*. Who is behind the way existence works, and for what purpose does it work that way? The prologue sets forth, with doxological precision, the ultimate implication for the whole of creation of God's universal purposes disclosed in the coming, death, and resurrection of Jesus Christ Lord. Christ is both the Eternal Word by whom all things were made and the Eternal Word who is the freely obedient fulfiller of the covenant in our — sinners' — stead. That is, Jesus Christ is Mediator of creation and Mediator of redemption.

It is difficult, I think, for many people today to hear the word "Word" in anything like its laminated Johannine meaning.[4] We are so accustomed to hearing "word" meaning a spoken utterance that the magnitude of the mystery of the incarnation is diminished to a language occurrence. Of course, "Word" also includes noise mouthed and tongued to express something; but even that implies something besides the noise, something to be expressed

---

4. Cf. below, in the section on the Word and para-verbal communication, in the chapter on the mystical body of Christ.

— emotion, alarm, idea, direction, and so on. When the tongued noise is part of a language spoken by a group, then a network of meaning, a context of sense, is in operation.

We have, above, described humans as questioning creatures. We could just as well have called humans linguistic creatures, in the sense that it is increasingly difficult to separate being human from the questing to express one's emotions and mental images. Now here is the crucial point: the mute are human, the silent are human, in their having a reality to express, whether that be by speaking or some other form of language, like body language, like artistic creativity, like pent-up anger, like upwelling tenderness, and so on. There is a reality, a set of realities, to be expressed — there to come forth as expression. The spoken word is but the vehicle through which this far larger reality becomes apparent, shows up, bursts forth. In other words (!), words, like unspoken words, are expressions of the Word.

Thought and speech presuppose corresponding minds and connectedness. The ancients spoke of this presupposed encompassing reality as *reason (Word, Logos)*. Reason is not primarily what we have in our heads, though its presence *also* there is what makes us "reasonable" and "rational." Reason is the universal mind — though some take it to be impersonal — behind and throughout all creation. Speech works because there is a microcosmic correspondence of signs among those thinking together and speaking together which itself is grounded in the macrocosmic correspondence between those signs and the universal realities to which they point. Some signs point more clearly to certain realities than other signs do. The aim of dialectic is to discover (or remember) which signs of thought and speech most approximate the realities to which they refer.

That is why Pythagoras is of such perennial interest and worth remembering. For him the nature of numbers is a key to more than mathematics, though it is also that. He thought that the nature of numbers is ultimately about the structure of the universe and of human thought and speech within that encompassing reality. We are probably more in agreement with him than we expect in our daily commerce. Whether or not we think about it, we operate on the basis of large rhetorical questions. Don't numbers refer to a reality? Don't formulae, say in astrophysics, refer to the way things really are "out there"? Don't those who are proudly empiricist still do their duplicatable experiments presupposing realities to which their actions correspond? Isn't mathematics a universal language? For that matter, isn't there a macrocosmic correspondence between the tones produced *here* by the vibrations of a string of a certain length and the same tones produced *there* by another string of the same length? Is this or that chord the same here and there, and if so, doesn't that imply a structure of reality that makes it so? All these matters are classical philosophical, physical questions, argued about by the cleverest minds of each era. They are perennial issues, agreement on which it is not necessary to gain for people to exercise their practical callings. However, just because they are complex or just because we should prefer to skip them, does not mean either that they will go away or that they are disposable assumptions.

Not long ago, we were dining with a specialist in number theory working at the Institute for Advanced Study. He was passionate about certain numbers and cold as a fish about others — a characteristic that is, so I have since learned, fairly common among number specialists. I have grown accustomed to the widespread nominalism which, in its modern attenuated form, thinks signs — words, symbols, numbers — do not refer to anything beyond customary usage, the cultural accumulation of sounds and ideas which get this or that response. But here was a mathematician as excited about numbers as astrophysicists are when a new set of "pictures" from the Hubble telescope is made available. I ventured the opinion that he was speaking about numbers as if they were "real things," not just culturally useful convention. He laughed and said that he and other mathematicians have to function on workdays as Platonists and Pythagoreans, but on Sunday they can be respectable modern agnostics about such implied metaphysics! He meant that we all work as if numbers are part of fundamental structures of the universe.

Now, a person may choose any of a number of symbols to account for the apparently perceived fundamental realities of the universe as far as we know it now — for the apparent de facto metaphysics implied in the exercise of our practical reason. And that choice of a symbol system (or, for those eclectically minded, a floating combination of several symbol systems) to account for this experienced presuppositional reality may well differ from those with which the prologue to John's Gospel works. Here all I am up to is spotting the conviction that, by whatever terminology, Jesus Christ, his person and his labor, is the clue, the key, the definitive and inclusive Mediator not just of redemption but also of creation.

The creed's operative conviction is that redemption and creation are finally not to be separated, and that Jesus Christ is the way creation and redemption are mutually defined and actualized. The Eternal Word is not abstract meaning, not the triumph of the keenest dialectic, not an angelic number or heavenly luminary. It turns out that the birth in the lowliest of circumstances means that the Eternal Word is known (in that participatory kind of knowing the Eternal Word himself evokes) as exactly the one who purposes goodness and beauty in creating and redeeming the other he has brought into being out of sheer overabundant love. Jesus Christ is not the best in a series. The many, the serial aspect to our lives, is a dependent reality, dependent on the uniqueness of the Eternal Word become flesh. That scandalous particularity of the universal meaning and reality of the universe — that is what the church had to fight for and which is testified to in the articles of the creed. Those fights were not mainly between believers and nonbelievers — there was plenty of that. The toughest fights, however, were among believers all seriously committed to getting right the faith of the church that they all sought to enhance.

Fully God

Brilliantly mistaken though the major erroneous teachers may have been on this or that aspect of the gospel, each was after a part of the truth; where they mainly erred was in the reduction of the breadth of affirmations held together by the gospel in its process of canonization. One of these thinkers who perhaps more than any of the others made sense to a wide range of people — and his teaching was defended by more people, longer than the others — was Arius. He taught that whatever else we say about God, it couldn't be at the expense of minimizing God's transcendence (as Arius understood, or misunderstood, transcendence). God is so other, so different, than creation — so Arius argued — that there could really be no point of contact, much less any kind of unity at all, between God and creation, much less God and the flesh in the incarnation. At the same time, Arius wanted to agree with the biblical claim that creation was the result of God's will, so Arius taught that the Word by whom all things were made was not fully God — was indeed godlike, but not fully God — and was, in effect, partly God and partly creature. The Word was thus — excuse the analogy — a kind of gear shift between God and creation, or to use another analogy, a kind of electrical transformer that reduced the voltage from the higher one to the lower one without burning the lower one out. According to Arius, it was in this sense — partly God and partly creature — that the Word was a Mediator of creation.

On Arius's scheme, we first find out what kind of God we are dealing with, then we ask how can such a God have any contact with creation and how can such a God be related to the human in the person Jesus Christ. That procedure makes a lot of sense. But the way the church eventually posed the question was very different: we do not really know what kind of God it is until we are confronted by his self-disclosure in the incarnation. God is defined by the incarnation, not the other way around. *Since* God meets us in the flesh of Jesus Christ born of Mary, *then* what kind of God do we discover is dealing with us? We discover God to be the one who hears the cry of those in Egypt and does something earthy about it. The one who sings with his people the Lord's song in a strange land. The one who knows each person while still in a mother's womb. The one to whom we cry from the deepest depths. The one who is the Servant Lord among us, Emmanuel. The one whose wisdom is foolishness to the world. In short, from the incarnation we discover God to be the one who mixes it up with and for the sake of all creatures great and small.

This alternative to Arius's commonsense way of posing the question is far more than a cognitive difference. The church's teaching on this point is, at root — radically — a difference of piety, of *eusebeia,* of ethos. It is a different morphology of freedom, a differentiating prodigality of praise. Ultimately the knowledge of God begins and grows with God's self-disclosure through the humanity of the Eternal Word. It is a lifelong, indeed eternity-long journey. It is growth in true happiness, of rejoicing in God's shared goodness, of expanding delight in the exulting society. It is moving upward, progression from plateau to plateau, ascent of the holy mountain following the steps of the one who for our sakes came down from heaven, who became poor that we through his poverty might become rich. This participation in God's knowledge of himself — and of ourselves within that love — is giving back to God God's movement toward us. God moves so far to us that God takes on the human condition without loss of — indeed, with fullness of — economy of creation and redemption. This mediation is not a matter of Christ's being partly divine and partly human — a *partly-partly* kind of bridging. It is a matter of Christ's being fully divine and fully human — a *fully-fully* kind of bridging. The latter, being simultaneously true God and true human — the *fully-fully mediation* — is one of a kind, not one of a series.

Fully Human

There is an altogether different option, and perhaps it is the earliest effort to state the relation between the human and the divine in Christ's makeup. It is the "appearance Christianity" mentioned above. You remember it is called Docetism from the Greek word for appearing. This option said that Christ only appeared to be human or only made his appearance in the form of a human, much like what is going on in the stories of the Greek gods and goddesses who can show up now as an owl or a ram or a person and so on.

This option was a natural attraction for early Christians because it was a readily accessible explanation in popular religion. On this basis God could appear in human form and leave it and not suffer either material defilement or pain on the cross: Christ only appeared to be human, as a kind of pedagogical enterprise, conveying worthwhile truths and performing startling miracles. Docetism obviated the teachings of the other intelligent options, orthodox and heterodox alike, by framing the question totally differently. Docetists did not have to struggle with the question of how the divine and the human were related in Christ, because technically there was no humanity which we share: there was only appearance. For example, Christ did not actually weep over

Jerusalem, nor was he really moved by the plight of Lazarus, nor was he really angry when overturning the tables before the temple, for such emotions were obviously unworthy of God who, above all — literally above all, including human emotions and physical fatigue and suffering — remained impassible.

As with the other options, it would be a mistake to think Docetism has disappeared. In fact, it may well be the most commonly held alternative. It makes sense if one has to do with a user-friendly deity and if the point of religion is to be related to the divine without the trammel of the earthy, temporal, corruptible dimensions of life. Three examples of Docetism's persistence in different forms will suffice.

First, when people are embarrassed by ancient editorial errors in the texts we have of books of the Bible, they often seem to suggest that Scripture's authority is dependent upon its freedom from human error. The idea is that the more we can get rid of the Scripture's culturally influenced humanness, the more we approach the "real" word of God behind, and despite, the human transmitters. In fact, of course, the very cultural humanness through which God encounters us belongs to the very nature of Scripture's being the written form of the Word of God. It is gluttony to lust for an ideal revelation supposedly devoid of cultural mediation.

Second, sentimental iconography or music — or art in any form which is sentimental — is nostalgia for times, places, persons unencumbered by the kinds of tragedies, ambiguities, conflicts that go unresolved in this life. Buechner identifies sentimentality. It is hunger for cost-free experience of intimacy — the desire to have the experience of an ideal world, one minus the grittiness of struggle where and when we are. "To sentimentalize something is to look only at the emotion in it and at the emotion it stirs in us rather than at the reality of it, which we are always tempted not to look at because reality, truth, silence are all what we are not very good at and avoid when we can. To sentimentalize something is to savor rather than to suffer the sadness of it, is to sigh over the prettiness of it rather than to tremble at the beauty of it, which may make fearsome demands of us or pose fearsome threats."[5]

I know that from time to time and from situation to situation the pain of people's lives drives them to hold on to whatever floating plank remains from the sinking ships of their lives. As a temporary coping technique, this is not the same as the programmatic escapism of much of sentimental art. I think of those pretty dreadful portrayals of Christ as a handsome Aryan matinee idol, or as an immaculate shepherd carrying pure white sheep and gliding down a garden path clad in a white gown just back from the Victorian cleaners. He only appears to be human. The sentimental modality longs for the purest-possible appearance of one not touched as we are. That is exactly the problem: sentimental art deprives us sinners and finite creatures of the assurance that comes from knowing Christ is the Mediator touched in every way as we all are, yet without sin.

Third, this same docetic attitude carries over into some views about the church. One form of this says simply, the less church the better. A person who bemoans the "institutional church," and instead wishes to have what is called a purely "spiritual" experience, is longing for salvation minus the mediating conditions of that wholeness. There is no human community without some sort of structure, no matter how minimal. Oh, indeed, "institutional church" can be used, by definition, to mean structures misused to protect the aggrandizing ways of self-perpetuating entitlement. In that case, of course, the prophets' message is sharply addressed against those who make religion into a lucrative instrument of class domination. But time and again the question is not whether the church is institution or not, but whether the church lives insti-

5. Frederick Buechner, *Listening to Your Life* (San Francisco: Harper, 1992), p. 104.

tutionally by the prophetic word and the freeing presence and activity of the Holy Spirit in a permanent state of revolution. This is a matter of more than semantics. It is a matter of how the prophetic word comes to us, how the gospel gets historically mediated, how the church struggles perennially to be the "according to the Word of God reforming church."

We touched on this above, but a reminder is in order here about another option that functioned to minimize Christ's full humanity. I refer to the teaching of Apollinaris. He was a follower of Athanasius, and so a staunch champion of the view that Christ was fully divine — of the same being as the Father. Apollinaris made the rather ingenious proposal that Jesus, like us, had a completely human body *(soma)* and a completely human soul *(psyche);* but unlike us, the God part of Jesus was his mind *(nous).* To put it far more crudely than the quite brilliant Apollinaris put it, Jesus Christ was two-thirds human and one-third divine. It was up to his sympathetic opponent, one of the famous Cappadocian triumvirate, Gregory Nazianzus, to formulate what was to prevail as the orthodox teaching. It is that Jesus Christ was *fully* human as well as fully divine. The reason for this, according to Gregory, is that whatever is not "taken up" — assumed — in the incarnation would not be healed — and for sure, our minds need healing as much as our souls and bodies do.

The Personal Union of God and Human Nature

As we have seen, when Nestorius came along, his view of Christ was well covered by the Nicene Creed in its 381 form. Nestorius taught that Christ was fully human and fully divine, but he balked at the implications of holding unflinchingly to the teaching that the two natures, human and divine, were *united* — not just closely attached, not just juxtaposed, not just concurrent, but *united.* For most of Nestorius's extensive ministry and work as a courageous bishop, this posed no problem. Then someone compared the way Mary was referred to in the liturgy Nestorius used in and around Antioch with the way Mary was referred to in the liturgy Cyril used in and around Alexandria. Nestorius could go no further than calling Mary the "Bearer of Christ" *(Christokos)*. Cyril went all the way and insisted that because the two natures were inseparably united even in the womb, Mary be called nothing less than the "Bearer of God" *(Theotokos)*.[6]

The differences were not just semantic: the debate exposed quite different tendencies in Antioch and Alexandria. However, for our shorthand purposes in these remarks on the creed, I am at this point only indicating that both Nestorius and Cyril were in agreement on the terms of the 381 formula. The task left undone by the 381 agreement had to be worked out later, in the Council of Ephesus, 431, and the Council of Chalcedon, 451. That is what is behind Luther's (some eleven centuries later) superb and (once the issue is posed) absolutely accurate hyperbole: "I neither have nor know any other God than this flesh which gestated in the womb of the Virgin Mary!"[7]

In some ways the most confusing (no pun intended) option was that advocated by Eutyches. If Nestorius erred in the direction of minimizing the union of the two natures, Eutyches went overboard so far in the other direction that he ended up confusing the two natures. The result, ironically enough, was a kind of amalgam in which the human and divine natures were lost. On this basis, so unique would be Christ's human nature that, were one to follow Eutyches' logic (to a place he chose not to go), the

6. For contemporary reflections on Mary from Protestant viewpoints, see Beverly Gaventa and Cynthia Rigby, eds., *The Blessed One: Protestant Perspectives on Mary* (Louisville: Westminster, 2002).

7. For Luther's and Calvin's specificity on this, see David Willis, *Calvin's Catholic Christology* (Leiden: Brill, 1966).

only human nature saved in the incarnation would be Christ's — which rather misses the point!

There was a long and vociferous debate about Eutyches' meaning. What is known as the single nature (Monophysite) controversy went on long after the fourth ecumenical council (Chalcedon, 451). At any rate, there was a kind of closure — to use some modern jargon — accomplished at the Council of Chalcedon. The major options were faced, and the four famous adverbs were accepted as sort of channel markers within which the doctrine of Christ's person and work would serve the unity of the church and not its divisions. The council used negative adverbs to affirm the positive identity of the one person Jesus Christ. Those adverbs were that the human and divine natures of Christ were united "without division, without confusion, without separation, without change."[8]

It is true that the Chalcedonian settlement was not looked upon as much of a settlement because even with the use of the four adverbs, there was still a good deal of latitude in the way Christ was thought of and worshiped. That was and is a great strength of the Chalcedonian decision: it is of sufficient breadth that it summarizes the doctrinal developments implicit in the Nicene decision of 325 and faces the major options for accounting for God's being among us humanly as Jesus Christ Lord. It took a stand about the perimeters of that development for the church's normative expression of the faith for worship and service.[9]

---

8. For the text of the decrees of 451, see Henry Bettenson, ed. and trans., *The Later Christian Fathers . . . a Selection . . . St. Cyril of Jerusalem to St. Leo the Great* (New York: Oxford University Press, 1970).

9. I shall not here go into christological development after Chalcedon, but I do want to alert my readers to the great elucidations that occurred with the writings, a century later, of Leontius of Byzantium. For the debate over whether Chalcedon was a unifying or a divisive formulation, and in what ways, see Paulos Gregorios, William Lazareth, and Nikos Nissiotis, eds., *Does Chalcedon Divide or*

There were and are, when it comes to the church's teaching about Christ, only a few major ways to speak about the mystery of the unity of God and humanity in the person of Christ. These major ways came to be defined as channel markers within which saving, sane, wholesome navigation could proceed. That is a very different picture from ones that either toss out the doctrinal development of this period altogether or treat the formations of these agreements as pretty much the last and fixed word. Channel markers for sane navigation are for proceeding. That means the dynamic business of discerning what the makers of the creed agreed to at the great ecumenical councils and then attempting to translate and interpret that agreement into the terms and ethics which serve the purposes of the gospel in subsequent languages and cultures.

The creedal language serves the gospel. When it has become so arcane for this or that culture, the creedal language does not need to be discarded but to be more faithfully transmitted, translated, and transfigured. The symbols have their *kairoi* over and again. The sacred symbols are not controlled by handlers, as if the hermeneutical process — this history of interpreting — were a rather mechanical business carried on by skilled communicators whose expertise is in audience analysis. Remember, we are here speaking about the mystery of the incarnation. Remember, we have said mystery means that which grows in its hiddenness the more we know it. The more we are caught up in its hiddenness, the more we are encountered in its disclosive power. To put the matter more simply and traditionally, the procedure of transmitting, translating, and transfiguring the creedal language is part of the work of the Holy Spirit.

Unite? Towards a Convergence in Orthodox Christology (Geneva: World Council of Churches, 1981). See also Iain Torrance, *Christology after Chalcedon: Severus of Antioch and Sergius the Monophysite* (Norwich: Canterbury Press, 1988).

The church in all its life lives by the power of the Spirit. That emphatically is the case with such a crucial matter as the church's seeking continually, from generation to generation, from culture to culture, to speak the truth in love. Once again we recall the difference between *believing something about* and *believing in*. Doctrine proceeds savingly when believers get on with the job of transmitting, translating, and transfiguring the creedal symbols which are guides to identifying Christ in whom we believe. In the subsequent history of witnessing to Christ doctrinally, the procedure itself is corrected, judged, revivified, and guided by the Holy Spirit *about whom we believe* something but primarily *in whom we believe*. This development of doctrine is part of the works prepared for us to walk in — by grace.

> But God, who is rich in mercy, out of the great love with which he loved us, even when we were dead through our trespasses, made us alive together with Christ (by grace you have been saved), and raised us up with him, and made us sit with him in the heavenly places in Christ Jesus, that in the coming ages he might show the immeasurable riches of his grace in kindness toward us in Christ Jesus. For by grace you have been saved through faith; and this is not your own doing, it is the gift of God — not because of works, lest any man should boast. For we are his workmanship, created in Christ Jesus for good works, which God prepared beforehand, that we should walk in them. (Eph. 2:4-10)

By way of summarizing this chapter, let me recall that the central doctrinal decision is that Jesus Christ is fully God, fully human, united into one person. The various options were possible ways of accounting for that reality. There was a development of doctrine in the sense that what was implicit in the Nicene decision of 325 was unfolded, made more explicit. That is, there was development of doctrine in the sense that what has been given once and for all gets elaborated in the face of threats to this razor's edge of grace, this radical simplicity of the central saving mystery. And yes, of course, this development of doctrine was immensely influenced by competing economic, social, political, psychological, and linguistic factors. So what else is to be expected in the treatment of precisely the fact that this God works through history and its relativities? That Jesus "suffered under Pontius Pilate" and died tells us the Word assumed a complete human being — in the ancients' language, body, mind, soul. This means the Mediator was — in the words of the book of Hebrews — tempted as we are in every way we are yet did not sin. He was obedient unto death, even that of crucifixion.

The razor's edge of grace is this confession: Jesus Christ is fully human, fully God, united in one person. Not two-thirds human and one-third divine, as Apollinaris is supposed to have taught. Not (as Nestorius is supposed to have taught) fully human and fully divine but not fully united into one person. Not (as Eutyches was supposed to have taught) with natures united in such a way that the reality of the two natures was threatened. The Chalcedonian adverbs serve as channel markers for safe worship and teaching. That is what it means to confess the mystery of the incarnation — the mystery to be lived adoringly as a reasonable wager that bears fruit in the common life of those like-minded.

Hear *theopoesis* on the sweep, boldness, costliness, cosmic context of wholeness.

[**A Man Who Had Fallen among Thieves**]
a man who had fallen among thieves
lay by the roadside on his back
dressed in fifteenthrate ideas
wearing a round jeer for a hat

fate per a somewhat more than less
emancipated evening
had in return for consciousness
endowed him with a changeless grin

whereon a dozen staunch and leal
citizens did graze at pause
then fired by hypercivic zeal
sought newer pastures or because

swaddled with a frozen brook
of pinkest vomit out of eyes
which noticed nobody he looked
as if he did not care to rise

one hand did nothing on the vest
its wideflung friend clenched weakly dirt
while the mute trouserfly confessed
a button solemnly inert.

Brushing from whom the stiffened puke
i put him all into my arms
and staggered banged with terror through
a million billion trillion stars[10]

---

10. e.e. cummings, "A Man Who Had Fallen among Thieves," in *Norton Anthology of Modern Poetry,* ed. Richard Ellmann and Robert O'Clair (New York: Norton, 1973), p. 532.

CHAPTER FIVE

The Work of Christ

✠   ✠

Through him all things were made. For us and for our salvation he came down from heaven: by the power of the Holy Spirit he became incarnate from the Virgin Mary, and was made man. For our sake he was crucified under Pontius Pilate; he suffered death and was buried. On the third day he rose again in accordance with the Scriptures; he ascended into heaven and is seated at the right hand of the Father. He will come again in glory to judge the living and the dead, and his kingdom will have no end.

For Us and Our Salvation

We will take this up again in the section on the one, holy, catholic, apostolic church, but the church is already presupposed in this part of the Nicene Creed. For it is in the church the confession of Christ's identity is made, and even more to the point, Christ's identity includes those he has called and united to himself by the power of the Holy Spirit. That is how Christ is savingly for us: through his body. Yes, through the body of the flesh taken from his mother Mary. However, also through the body of those he has called and who believe in him. This is the "society of divine happiness," as Edwards calls the church.

Today, one of the most unpopular claims a person or a group can make is that he or she or they are chosen. That does not mean that people do not consider themselves or their nation or family chosen. It is just that they are hungry to define their chosenness (election) in a nonsuperior-sounding way. They would rather define their specialness in terms of their own achievements. There is a good reason for that. They do not want to perpetuate destructive claims to entitlement and special privilege based on race or wealth or education or family background or nationality. This gets sticky because the biblical material is loaded with the claims the people of God, Old Testament and New, make about their experience of being chosen, called out, consecrated, and designated as a holy community. The thing that saves these claims from elaborate self-serving aggrandizement is that the people of God are set apart, called out *(ek kaleo: ecclesia)* not for privilege but for service, empowered not for domination but for servanthood. That is part of the scandal of the gospel. Being united to the Servant Lord is to be committed to serve after the manner of his obedience unto the death of the cross. Hence the foot washing by Christ of the disciples. That is why Christians are indeed chosen — chosen for service of God's purposes in the grittiness and beauty of this world. Participation in the chosen one means to share in his victorious service.

The victory of the cross is not of the kind of triumph we usually think of. We usually think of victory as the putting down and destruction of one's enemies. That is also part of the imagery of redemption: death, sin, and the devil are put under Christ's feet, and the heel of Mary's seed bruises the serpent's head, and the Lamb drives the beast away. The triumph of the cross is all that — and more. The more is a continuation of the scandal. Here enemies are forgiven and those united to the Servant Lord are commanded to pray for those enemies, to forgive them even — or especially — when they mean them harm, to love after the manner of the one who did not sin or deserve death but took that infinitely costly suffering — the consequences of sin — unto himself. We share in his singular redemptive suffering, but our suffering is not the redemptive one.

"Redemptive suffering" is a dangerous term and must be used with as much care as daring. For all suffering is not redemptive, nor is suffering in itself redemptive. There is a plague that seeks to assure oneself of one's election by the prominence of one's suffering. That form of works righteousness is as virulent as the effort to assure oneself of one's election by the prominence of one's so-called successes. Suffering comes naturally. None, believer or not, is exempt from it, and none, with one exception, really can know the suffering of another person. The black spiritual has it right: "Nobody knows the suffering I've seen; nobody knows but Jesus." There is an additional dimension, however, of costliness for those who are blessed in suffering for righteousness' sake. Seeking righteousness is accompanied by costly living, but costly living is not a way of earning righteousness. Pursuing righteousness brings its own consequences. If you believe in the gospel and its demands, you don't have to go looking for that kind of trouble. It goes with the territory of belonging to the one who ushers in the Day of the Lord. If anyone would follow Jesus, that one must also follow in the way of the Lord's self-giving love.

That is what is behind the reality of a specific kind of sacrificial love: of giving oneself for others. The language of sacrifice is not the only way of expressing how wholeness is mediated to us, but it is part of the richness of the biblical eloquence. I will presently say more about this imagery. Here, however, we need to insist on the main point in the way priestly sacrifice is handled in the book of Hebrews: whatever sacrifice is necessary, in that interpretive framework, has been offered by the all-sufficient High Priest,

Jesus Christ. *We are Christ's but we are not christs.* Christ's once-for-all (Heb. 7:23-28) sacrifice frees us from messianic complexes and burdens. His once-for-all person and work save us from the necessity of being the Messiah, the messiah of our own fictitious but destructive expectations for the sins of the whole world — and from the messianic expectations others may place upon us. Hence the wisdom of that part of the liturgy that refers to the "one, full and complete sacrifice" for the sins of the whole world: *Agnus Dei qui tollet peccata* <u>*mundi*</u>. It is that singular sacrifice which frees the congregation to offer, as part of their *eucharistia,* thanksgiving, themselves, souls and bodies to be a living sacrifice.

The Motion of Salvation

For us and our salvation, Christ came down and ascended. He took on our humanity, was obedient unto death in it, raised it to new life in his victory, and will come again in it. That parabolic movement is the shape of salvation, the shape of the humiliation and the exaltation of the Eternal Word enhumaned, Jesus Christ. Our salvation is in his joining us to himself by the power of the Spirit in this movement. The descent was no playacting by someone who knew in advance how things were going to turn out. That would give in to the docetic temptation again. The incarnate Word was tested, struggled, accomplished a costly victory. The Mediator was really tested in all points as we are, yet did not share our systemic rejection of God. There is no corner of the human story, no corner of despair or joy, where the Mediator of creation has not also functioned for us as the Mediator of salvation. Through the stories shaped by the resurrection, we acknowledge that we too share Christ's victory in the depths.

For *us* he came down. That means he did not come down for himself. He did not need saving. If there is any necessity here, it is the irresistibility of divine compassion. It is the nature of sovereign love to be near, to care for, to take pity on loved ones. If we who are so imperfect and capricious know to give our loved ones care, how much more does God care and do something about the plight of those in bondage to sickness, starvation, loneliness, indignity, cruelty — you name it. Taking on our cause is an action of sheer grace, an unwarranted gift, the gift of God's own self.

We know very little about where he came down from and ascended to. The parlance for this is brief, evocative, and tautological. He "came down" from the "realms of glory," from "heaven," from "on high." He "ascended" "on high," to "the right hand of the Father," and so on. The point is not to try to make this movement fit an ancient Middle East cosmology. That imagery is for conveying something more essential. It has to do with the struggle to right what is wrong. It has centrally to do with the happiness of justice, as equanimous love triumphing over the ingenuity of hate. It has to do with the vindication of the most life-filled peace, a peace that is in fact far, far beyond our wildest dreams of happiness. That we cannot imagine its extent and intricacy is part of the point of the vision of descent from and return to the realms of glory. Glory is redefined by this victorious humility. The greatest glory is manifest in God's freedom and power, the costly love that restores the right ordering and freeing of creatures gone astray. The realms of glory are not left behind but relocated to include what is already lived out here and now by the Mediator whose perfect obedience is in lieu of our choices of death over life.

Here, once again, we confront the paradox we have noted before: the full plight of humanity is known from the experience of its being overcome. It is only when we are assured of salvation that we can look our demons in the eye. That is what it means to say we have the courage that comes from being clothed in the garment of Christ's righteousness. Repentance fully comes only with the shock of realizing the love that undergirds our whole being.

That experience of repentance grows more and more in direct proportion to our discovering more and more the ingenuity of sovereign love.

There is a reason that the first time the Nicene Creed explicitly refers to the condition of sin is when it confesses that Christ came down for our *salvation*. Salvation defines sin, not the other way around. What we are saved for is clearer and more powerful than what we are *saved from*. Indeed, it is only when we get to the third article of the creed that sin is mentioned explicitly. Even then, as we shall see, sins are introduced as what we are baptized into the forgiveness of. That is bad syntax, I know; but it is permissible here to make the point that sin is taken so seriously that it is defined as that which it cost God's own redemptive suffering to forgive, to take away. Sin does not go away of its own accord. That is why we sing, using John the Baptizer's libretto, "Behold, the Lamb of God, who takes away the sin of the world!" (John 1:29).

Under Pontius Pilate Crucified, Suffered Death, Was Buried

We have already noted many of the images, the language, the "symbols" which abound in Scripture to describe the various manifestations of the fact of redemption. Sacrifice is one, victory another, unity of believers to Christ another, incarnation another, servant Lordship another, and so on. Where the church got in trouble in its treatment of atonement or redemption — I use the terms synonymously — was when it emphasized only one at the expense of the others. The gospel has an accommodating and transforming strength. In different cultures, different images naturally suggested themselves more than others. It is part of the power of the gospel that it appropriated terms and imagery of this or that culture and broke them open and filled them with a radically different content, precisely so that the scandal was that of the gospel and not a false scandal of indifferent things.

Gustav Aulen, in his influential book *Christus Victor*,[1] argued that there are three main ways of looking at Christ's saving work: the moral influence theory (most associated with Abelard), the substitutionary or propitiatory theory (most associated with Anselm), and what he calls the classic theory (the one he favors, hence the title of his book), which describes redemption as battle and victory through cross and resurrection. In fact, each representative theologian (Anselm, Abelard, Athanasius) has large chunks of all three types in his writings. Aulen's types have become commonplace by now and are often used without his nuance. They are useful as long as we remember they were never intended to be exhaustive.

There are other strong types that prevent serious reduction of the range of biblically warranted imagery. I think especially of healing, or restoration of the beauty of creation, or reparation of the image of God, or restoration of the right relation between body and soul, or correction and renewal of God-instilled reason. So when one is tempted to say which theology of redemption best suits the biblical and creedal material for thinking and speaking of the redemptive work of Christ, the only accurate thing is to say yes to each and all of the above.[2] The most impoverishing thing is to reduce the imagery to only one or two, into which

1. Gustav Aulen, *Christus Victor* (New York: Macmillan, 1951).

2. Among the most helpful and accessible treatments of this range, see Leanne Van Dyk, *The Desire of Divine Love: John McLeod Campbell's Doctrine of the Atonement* (New York: P. Lang, 1995); Bruce L. McCormack, *For Us and Our Salvation: Incarnation and Atonement in the Reformed Tradition,* Studies in Reformed Theology and History (Princeton: Princeton Theological Seminary, 1993); Frederick W. Dillistone, *Christian Understanding of the Atonement* (Philadelphia: Westminster, 1968); and of course, paragraphs 59, 64, and 69 of Karl Barth, *Church Dogmatics* IV/1, IV/2, and IV/3 respectively; see Barth, *Church Dogmatics* I/1–IV/4 (Edinburgh: T. & T. Clark, 1936-69).

danger individual theologians fell from time to time. Here Tillich is wise when he speaks of the range of symbols each with its own power and own timeliness *(kairos),* all of which are to be kept, even — or perhaps especially — when any given symbol seems most out of date and irrelevant.

There are various *theories* of the atonement or reconciliation. That statement means two things. First, it would be nice if atonement came from "at-one-ment," but that is a bit of linguistic coincidence. Atonement comes from the verb "to atone," and that means to make up for, to do something to repay for, to give satisfaction. The term "atonement" therefore already has a connotation of giving satisfaction for something, making up for some failure or offense or hurt. Often, though, "atonement" is spoken of as more general than the satisfaction model, as when we speak of various theories of the atonement.

It is a bit clearer, I think, to speak about *various theories of reconciliation,* of which atonement is one. Reconciliation is broader than atonement. Reconciliation has the connotation of mediation between two parties — what a mediator brings about. It means bridging the gap of alienation, overcoming the estrangement that gets in the way of enjoying the benefits of God's unstinting love. Not accepting the freely and lavishly given love is a dreadful offense, a paralyzing bargaining for what is already opulently extended — ours for the taking. Reconciliation therefore also includes the sense of getting put right an offense against God's sovereign love.

Indeed, we are saved from a condition, but that condition is *not* our finiteness. It is more than finitude that alienates us from God. In fact, as Reinhold Niebuhr was wont to say, sin is mainly a matter of refusing to accept our finitude, plus the consequences of that refusal.[3] Our finitude is part of the goodness of our

---

3. Reinhold Niebuhr, *The Nature and Destiny of Man* (New York: Charles Scribner's Sons, 1955).

creatureliness. We are being saved not from our finitude but from our hankering to be at the center of our and others' universes — in short, our hankering to be the Highest Good. Luther, among others, called this condition "being curved in on self." It is the condition of considering oneself "entitled." It is ascribing to self a status that supposedly exempts one from the accountabilities and ordinariness that apply to the run-of-the-mill humans.

This condition is all the more dangerous for its ubiquity and its ability to take the noblest disguises: I am charmingly, or religiously, or most meekly, the beneficiary of entitlement — which, of course, I use for the well-being of others! Reconciliation is the overcoming of all that arrests our development into the maturity God intends and that is visible in the face of Christ. That, as we shall see, has to do with forgiveness.

Second, the theories of reconciliation are just that: theories. A theory is different from a saving doctrine, a defined dogma of the church. A theory in theological discourse is not exactly like a conjecture in mathematics, but it is close in the sense that its formulation is an attempt to account for the way a truth behaves. I know that is a curious expression: a truth that behaves. I mean, however, that the magnitude of the freedom, the new direction of energy, and the joy that come from the new life in Christ are such that the very singularity of the event evokes a rich variety of responses and interpretations. A latitude of images is called on to address the existential question, "What is going on and why is it going on?" There is a cultural richness in the Old and New Testaments that finds expression in a plethora of imagination to point to, to approximate, the transformation being experienced at the hands of God.

When we spoke above of *the mystery of the incarnation,* we referred to the positive content of the term "mystery." Mystery is reality too deep to be exhausted by our knowing, but it evokes that corresponding deep knowing. Mystery in this sense is not the result of an absence of knowing. The mystery known is too deep for enclosure in our thought and language. We have to speak the same way of *the mystery of reconciliation.* We indeed have words and emotions and thoughts for the mystery of reconciliation. However, the language and thought tools are reliable, sufficient pointers only because their subject, the holy one, makes them to refer to the reality too deep to be enclosed in any combination of formulations.

The Cross and False Stumbling Blocks

Of all the symbols pointing to the reality of Christ's saving presence and work, substitutionary atonement seems the one most open to misconstrual. This is also called the propitiation theory. Notice that it is a theory alongside other theories. It magnifies those parts of the Bible that do indeed draw heavily on the imagery of a lamb or other innocent beast being sacrificed to appease God, the cost of purification being the blood of the sacrificial offering. Anselm drew on this imagery,[4] but changed it to fit the feudal currency of a debt owed God by a rebellious subject. Christ's suffering compensated for our sin against the divine majesty. What we, because of our sin, owed God and could not pay, Christ paid for us.

I find it difficult to defend this view of the atonement. However, because it is part — if only a part — of the wide range of ways the Bible speaks about Christ's saving work, there is good reason for seeing some deeper issues in this imagery. I mention only three things in its favor.

First, and one we have already touched on, it is biblical. Even if we find it most offensive, it still has a claim to our critical atten-

4. Anselm of Canterbury, "Why God Became Man," in *A Scholastic Miscellany,* ed. Eugene R. Fairweather (Philadelphia: Westminster, 1956), pp. 100-183.

tion. Otherwise we make up our own canon on the basis of the shifting cultural sands and are tempted to miss some perennial truths to which the biblical material holds our otherwise too delicate noses.

Second, there is an archetypal reason for the prominence of this language of suffering on behalf of another person, and suffering that is not just educational but entails appeasement. That is Jung's point about our shadow sides: they are aspects of our unconscious which, if left buried and unfaced, function destructively to impede maturation. There seems to be a primordial, cross-cultural demand for justice in the crude form of repayment in kind. This is the *lex talionis:* an eye for an eye, a tooth for a tooth, a costly sacrifice for a costly hurt, an appeasement fitting the size of the insult, and so on. Gilbert and Sullivan did not make up the idea that the punishment should fit the crime. We see that all the time: when families on television relax and are satisfied that "justice has been done" only when the murderer of their relative has been executed; when each side in the Middle East or in Northern Ireland persists in mutually destructive escalation of retaliatory justice; when the offended party in a marital dispute insists that the other pay for the hurt done before any reconciliation is possible; when people react with glee when someone they think has gotten too uppity stumbles from favor and so "gets what is coming" to her or him.

Now, so long as this primordial demand for a cost to be paid for restoration and justice cries out in the psyche, that hunger needs directing, channeling, into constructive ways. Mainly, that means it needs channeling into ways of assuring persons of their forgiveness, assuring people that guilt has been faced and effectively taken care of, assuring them that whatever cost they need to see paid to experience pardon has been paid on the offending one's behalf. It mainly means assuring people that the punishment for injustice, of which guilt is the sign, has been accomplished.

One may well wish that the shadow side which demands an eye for an eye be exposed and transformed. In the meantime, however, it may well be that part of the earthiness of the vessel in which the treasure of the gospel comes to people is the imagery of substitutionary appeasement. That is quite different from saying that God has to be appeased. It is, on this interpretation, saying that our all-too-human conception of justice is what is appeased — our sense of justice is offended by the unfairness which comes with flaunting what our consciences tell us is profoundly wrong, whereas if we learn anything from Christ's teaching and ministry it is that God's justice is not that of humans.

Third, the substitutionary theory is put in perspective by radically extending the insight that it is by the whole course of Christ's obedience — *beginning with the incarnation* — that we are saved. I take my cue from Calvin when he says that Christ redeemed us by the whole course of his obedience, including his incarnation. That is, Calvin does not speak of the incarnation and the atonement as if they were two separate actions. Rather — as we suggested above — Christ's whole obedience constitutes a restoring and healing trajectory. It is God's parabolic movement from on high into history and thence, taking up the human condition, vindication in resurrection and ascension.

This saving and re-creating movement is a trinitarian choice of love. It is the way of God's choosing to be for us from before the foundation of the world. The incarnation is not an afterthought. God knew what God was getting into in creating. He knew the risk of creating creatures with the capacity for accepting love and the capacity of rejecting love. God knew the way into the distant land of alienation and the way home to free, trusting, joyful obedience born of love.

That obedience of Christ takes him to the cross. The agonizing death of the one pure creature exposes the fact that life as we know it is — to put it mildly — not fair. It is also the gross unfairness, the infuriating injustice, of the world that Christ also takes on in the incarnation. That action is part of the prophetic office of the incarnate one. It is prophetic activity to live faithfully and to seek justice in *this unfair world,* where injustice is as often as not perpetuated in the best of circumstances, to say nothing of the worst. Christ came into *this* world, not into an idealized world. It is in this way — of Christ's being the fulfiller of the covenant from both sides, God's and humanity's — that Christ is representative.

The incarnation is the Eternal Word's assumption, taking up, the full humanity, mind, body, soul, on the grounds that what is not thus taken on is not redeemed. The human condition includes the social memory — the symbol system, if you will — of a people, so that the flesh the Eternal Word took from the virgin Mary included the imagery by which faithful Israel conceived of how cleansing, purification, atonement, assurance of pardon became effective for us. That imagery included the sacrificial system whereby an innocent creature was the scapegoat who carried the sins of the people off into the wilderness. The idea that God needs to be appeased belonged to that imagery. Christ took that part of Israel's humanity onto the cross and into the grave as part of that which died in his death so that it no longer has mordant power over us.

The event of cross and resurrection sounds the death knell of the perverted understanding of God's fidelity which conceives of the Father needing to be appeased by the suffering and death of the Son — much as was the point of the aborted sacrifice of Abraham's son. I can see no way of holding together two utterly contradictory convictions, namely, (a) that God is not only loving but is love, and (b) that God needs to be appeased by the death of his only-begotten Son. Trying, finally, to hold those two views of God's nature, or so it seems to me, is to keep in place a false stumbling block, a supposedly required belief which in fact causes people to twist way out of shape the by-far-dominant teaching of the

New — and Old — Testament. That vastly dominant truth is that God's loving includes both the fact of reconciliation and the way reconciliation was accomplished. The ends and means of God's love are congruent. Through Christ's person and work we come to the assurance that we have never fallen from God's love.

The resurrection of the incarnate Word does not mean the annihilation of the old humanity that Christ took up.[5] It means its radical transformation — or, to be more technical, its transfiguration. The old conception of the Father's needing to be appeased is rejected by Christ's sacrifice once and for all. It does not need to be repeated. This conception has done its most, expended its energy in the ultimate sacrifice, which is Christ's.

In the resurrection the whole system of substitutionary atonement was transfigured. It gets subsumed under the loving act of God in choosing to become human and being obedient in fulfilling the covenant in our stead. Covenantal fulfillment is not equivalent to propitiatory sacrifice. At its deepest level, fulfilling the covenant has to do with the doing of justice, not with perpetuating a view of God as unjust cosmic bully. In Christ's establishing solidarity with the many, with the downtrodden and oppressed, with the blind and lame and leprous, he is doing the justice which the faithfully covenanting God requires. The atonement is not a transaction which occurs over our heads and behind our backs. It has to do with Christ's freeing us as members of his body to manifest God's *love* in the doing of justice. The substitutionary language has its place, but its place is part of the whole sweep of God's redeeming and re-creating ways in Christ's presence and work. It makes for unhealthy theology when we

5. For this see James B. Torrance, "The Vicarious Humanity of Christ," in *The Incarnation*, ed. Thomas F. Torrance (Edinburgh: Handsel Press, 1981), chap. 6, and Garret Dawson's fresh study on the ascension, *Jesus Ascended* (London/New York: T&T Clark International, 2002).

keep skipping verses of the great hymns just to shorten the service. The following needs singing all the way through.

1. The Babe in Bethlem's manger laid,
   In humble form so low;
   By wond'ring Angels is survey'd
   Thro' all His scenes of woe.

   > **Chorus**
   > Nowell, Nowell,
   > Now sing a Saviour's birth;
   > All hail, all hail
   > His Coming down to earth,
   > Who raises us to Heav'n!

2. A Saviour! sinners all around
   Sing, shout the wondrous word.;
   Let every bosom hail the sound,
   A Saviour! Christ the Lord. **Chorus**

3. For not to sit on David's throne
   With worldly pomp and joy,
   He came for sinners to atone
   And Satan to destroy. **Chorus**

4. To preach the Word of Life Divine,
   And feed with living Bread,
   To heal the sick with hand benign,
   And raise to life the dead. **Chorus**

5. He preached, He suffered, bled and died,
   Uplift 'twixt earth and skies;
   In sinners' stead was crucified,
   For sin a sacrifice. **Chorus**

6. Well may we sing a Saviour's Birth,
   Who need the Grace so given,
   And hail His coming down to earth,
   Who raises His to Heaven. **Chorus**

Rose Again according to the Scriptures

We have been speaking about the various theories of the atonement as "symbols," a usage which makes me uncomfortable because often today a symbol is what you have instead of the reality. I need here to repeat: when I (and here I am following Tillich) use "symbols," I mean signs that participate in the reality to which they point. For Tillich, even the understanding of God as love in a personal way is such a symbol. The personal qualities we use to conceive and speak of God as love are true because they point to the reality in which they participate.

The definitive instance of this is the resurrection. No one knows the details of that raising of Christ Jesus from the dead. There is not sequential photography like the early photos of people running in frame after frame. That is part of the point: we are excluded from the intimacy of that act of raising Christ Jesus from the dead. The disciples experience the real presence of the living Lord, not the details of how he got raised. But what the disciples experience is not their experience of their experience and so on: they experience the reality, which moves them to remember and proclaim the resurrection.

Tillich maintains that the resurrection is a historical event because it is comprised of *happening* with *interpretation*.[6] Historical

---

6. See Alexander J. McKelway, *The Systematic Theology of Paul Tillich* (Richmond, Va.: John Knox, 1964), pp. 168ff., on senses in which cross and resurrection are "historical" for Tillich.

event means just that: a happening mediated through interpretation. That is quite different from considering the resurrection as the first instance of the Easter faith, just a subjective (it is also subjective, but there is also a prior objective pole to it) experience of — what? — of the disciples' own faith. Here, all I am trying to make as clear and as brief as possible is that the atonement consists of the whole course of Christ's obedience, the whole sweep of the redeeming person, presence, and work of the Eternal Word become flesh — and that this redeeming movement is the result of God's eternal love, not a love the Father began to have when appeased.

Here we need to repeat the paradox we have noted before: it is from the good news that we know the extent of what might have been the bad news as the overall reality. It is from being saved that we know with any accuracy what it is we are saved from. That is true of the historical character of the event of the resurrection. By the resurrection in the singular I mean Christ's being raised from the dead, his ascension from the depths, his vindication as the promised Messiah. The resurrection is the presupposition of accurately pointing to the whole course of Christ's obedience.

It is because the risen Christ confronts us that we recognize who it was who did what he did. His identity as the risen, confronting Christ is the presupposition of our knowing his deeds to be saving. We will say something more about the dynamics of this being encountered by the risen Christ when we take up the third article, that on the person and work of the Holy Spirit — and of the community of believers Christ joins to himself by the power of the Holy Spirit. It suffices here to remind ourselves that we know what the resurrection is from being confronted by the risen Christ.

Our modern problem is how we can know Christ is raised from the dead. The disciples' problem was how it can be that

Christ is raised from the dead but not others at the same time. In some quarters the resurrection at the end of the times was expected. Indeed, a general resurrection was to be the main event of the final vindication of God's purposes. That general resurrection was, by some expectations, to be so that all may appear before the judgment seat of God. We get some glimpses of that expected general resurrection in the Gospel which speaks of the graves being opened and the formerly dead being seen walking around when the veil of the temple is rent from top to bottom at Christ's death. Even in that passage, note that Christ's own death is what opens graves and makes others to be alive.

That is also reflected in the predicament Lazarus faces. He dies but is raised again — and so, in effect, he is more a marked man than he was before he died. The issue is that if he was really raised from the dead by Jesus, he is a walking proof of Jesus' identity as the Messiah. The same expectation of a general resurrection seems to be in the background when Christ is referred to as the firstfruits of many such raisings from the dead. That is at least what Paul is also about when he turns the general apocalyptic expectation to the continued existence of the earth and people; those who share in Christ's death also share in his resurrection. It is now not so much the plurality of resurrections that is our hope, but exactly our participation in the singularity of Christ's resurrection.

Luke 24 provides a paradigm of what it means to be encountered by the risen Christ. It is a rich chapter with layered senses, of which I intend to mention only three.

First, one of the more curious and important parts of the narrative is that the disciples are accompanying the risen Christ on the road to Emmaus and do not know who he is until later. As they walk, this stranger opens up all of Scripture — the Old Testament, in our terms — that has to do with himself. His fellow travelers still do not make the connection. Apparently this hidden character of Christ's presence is an essential ingredient of the narrative. Here we have another instance of the hidden-revealed character of the divine encounter. There is no revelation that is not that of hiddenness, and the hiddenness is that of God personally self-disclosing. This is no more a mind twister than the necessity of saying of light that it is both particle and wave. You do not have the one without the other, and if you have only the one you don't really have even that.

Second, part of the contents of the encounter on the road to Emmaus is the continuity-discontinuity nature of the resurrection. God's continuous fidelity takes the shape of radical discontinuity. Death means cessation of life, stopping life, finality, terminus, nothingness. Resurrection means coming to life again, getting up and being about, newness, novelty, re-beginning. There is no easy transition from one to the other. There is, indeed, no material of such an end and new beginning — no field, as it were — except the hiddenness of the *triduum sacrum,* the holy three days of cross, of bursting the bonds of hell, and of resurrection. All we know is that defeat was turned to triumph, nothingness into new beginning.

Third, it is in the breaking of bread that the eyes of the disciples are opened and they recognize Jesus — recognize the encountering one to be the crucified one. In the history of interpretation, this breaking of the bread has been taken to be a reference to an early eucharistic practice. You may even have a glimmer of the angels, if that is what they were, who figure in the annunciation to Sarah. Be that as it may, traditional courtesy is shown a stranger. The obligation to offer hospitality to a stranger becomes the occasion for the disciples' realization of who has been dealing with them. The day is "far spent," and they want Jesus to stay with them. There is a warmly human side to this story — what else? I mean there is a note of affection, of caring, that shows through in this incident — not just an obedience to a law about offering hospitality. The breaking of bread is an ordinary courtesy, and that ordinariness becomes the culmination of this particular divine-human encounter. It is not the breaking of the bread that makes it a holy encounter. It is the presence of the holy one that makes the breaking of the bread revelatory.

Lest we miss the point, the narrative again underlines the hiddenness of the disclosive event. After the recognition, the boundary is again drawn and the manifest one is the hidden one. A psychosocial trick is not going on; rather, the veil is in place again. Efforts to explain the disappearance from the disciples' eyes miss the hidden-disclosed character of the encountering of the risen Christ. By the time the disciples have run back up — and it is way uphill — to the room where other disciples are gathered, Christ has already appeared to them. Note well the great fact that among those gathered were some "who disbelieved for joy."

The resurrection accounts were written after the fact and after the coming of the Holy Spirit on many. That is to say that the narratives themselves are shaped by the presence and activity of the Holy Spirit, to which we will presently turn. Before we do that, however, an additional word is necessary about the connection between the event of the resurrection and those who were the chosen witnesses. Here I reiterate what we noted above. I find Tillich's definition of a historical event useful: a happening to which we have access only through its interpretation. By that Tillich refuses to empty happening from any content, as, for example, by reducing the resurrection to an Easter awakening of the disciples' faith. The happening part of the event is what compelled the disciples to be confronted by a reality that demands interpretation.

The corollary of this is that the apostolic interpretation of the happening is part of the historical event. The risen Christ comes to the community of interpretation in such a way that it, the interpretive and proclaiming community, is part of how Christ is for us. We shall see the import of that when, in chapter 6, we turn to the doctrine of "the whole Christ." That is the doctrine that the reality in whom we participate by the power of the Holy Spirit is not Christ alone (a hypothetical idea anyway) but Christ joined to the members of his body. It is by the power of the Holy Spirit that this union is effected. We now turn to what the Nicene Creed has to say about the person and work of the Holy Spirit.

CHAPTER SIX

God the Holy Spirit

✠   ✠

One of the things that make the creed of 381 the most ecumenical is that its treatment of the Holy Spirit is fuller than either the Apostles' Creed or the creed of 325. The language of the latter is explosively simple: "And in the Holy Spirit." It is explosive in the sense that confessing belief in the Holy Spirit entails an acknowledgment of the Spirit's full divinity, matching the confession of the godness of the Father and the Son. As with Christology, the fuller statement is an unfolding of what was implicit in the earlier creedal form. That, in turn, was implicit in the biblical claims about the people of God's *experience* of the Holy Spirit. I use the term "experience" here deliberately and with benevolence aforethought. To know God is to enjoy his benefits. That applies no less to the Holy Spirit than to the Father and the Son. The proper knowledge of the Holy Spirit is the enjoyment of the presence and activity of the Holy Spirit in creation and redemption.[1] The

---

1. Obviously, again the resources for studying further the person and work of the Holy Spirit are rich, for which I mention here only Yves Congar, *I Believe in the Holy Spirit* (New York: Seabury Press, 1983); Michael Welker, *God the Spirit* (Minneapolis: Fortress, 1994); and above all, Karl Barth, *Church Dogmatics* IV/1, par. 58, for an overview of the Holy Spirit in the doctrine of reconciliation. Barth, *Church Dogmatics* I/1–IV/4 (Edinburgh: T. & T. Clark, 1936-69).

Holy Spirit is *Creator Spiritus* and *Redemptor Spiritus,* two sides of the very same reality who wills to be known experientially.

Here we have a parallel to the confession about the inseparability of God's work of creation and of redemption — buttressed by the fact that we cannot, should not, consider nature abstracted from that part of nature which is human nature. The creating work of the Holy Spirit is inseparable from the redeeming work of the Holy Spirit. The Holy Spirit calls us, principally through the Word, to transforming repentance for our sake and for the sake of the earth — indeed, for the entire part of the universe within the range of human dalliance. As is his wont, Gerard Manley Hopkins is clearheaded on this matter.

God's Grandeur
The world is charged with the grandeur of God.
    It will flame out, like shining from shook foil;
    It gathers to a greatness, like the ooze of oil
Crushed. Why do men then now not reck his rod?
Generations have trod, have trod, have trod;
    And all is seared with trade; bleared, smeared with toil;
    And wears man's smudge and shares man's smell: the soil
Is bare now, nor can foot feel, being shod.

And for all this, nature is never spent;
    There lives the dearest freshness deep down things;
And though the last lights off the black West went
    Oh, morning, at the brown brink eastward, springs —
Because the Holy Ghost over the bent
    World broods with warm breast and with ah! bright wings.[2]

---

2. Gerard Manley Hopkins, "God's Grandeur," in *The Norton Anthology of Modern Poetry,* ed. Richard Ellmann and Robert O'Clair (New York: Norton, 1973), p. 80.

The Holy Spirit is not our experience. The Holy Spirit is God. The Holy Spirit freely chooses to make herself experienced. The Holy Spirit transcends any set experience of herself or himself. The sovereignty of the Holy Spirit is, however, the opposite of caprice. The Holy Spirit is reliably, trustworthily behind our experience.[3] God the Spirit freshly chooses to be the loving referent of our experience. The Holy Spirit is to be trusted, counted on, believed in, confessed in the creed, delighted in, prayed for and to, and heartily obeyed. *Veni Creator et Redemptor Spiritus!*

In this respect there is a parallel to what we noted about the transcending presence of the Eternal Word who is united to the flesh but not restricted to it, who makes himself to be experienced by us but who is thereby not restricted to our experience. We experience the Eternal Word and the Holy Spirit because God remains God in being for us. We experience more than our experience of our experience of our experience and so on. The reality that grasps us is infinitely greater than ourselves. By it we are freed for becoming, day by day, more and more, our truest selves.

The discovery of this new freedom is no smooth business.[4] We undergo the death of the old self and the birth pangs of the new. We live more and more as persons created and restored in the image of God. That is costly. It means engaging in a discipline of loving service. It is a conversion of delight, a newly found spontaneity in caring for others and self. This new delight is forgetful of the cost. We are *converted from* self-conscious service and *converted to* doing what comes naturally as people moved by acceptance, not threat, moved by good news rather than by fear of not

3. For clarification of senses of "experience," see Louis W. Mitchell, *Jonathan Edwards on the Experience of Beauty* (Princeton: Princeton Theological Seminary, 2003).

4. See James Loder's treatment of this in his *The Transforming Moment* (San Francisco: Harper and Row, 1981). See also Barth's treatment of conversion in *Church Dogmatics* IV/2, par. 66.4.

being noticed and appreciated. When Augustine counseled that we are to love God and do what we will, he meant that when our love is refocused from self to God, then "what we have a taste for" is fundamentally altered. The freedom to be oneself comes, but comes only as a consequence of converted delight. Then I am freed for sane self-love, freed for nurturing the new self I have discovered I want to become.

This conversion of delight is just another expression of the life lived not by the law but by the gospel. Grace restores the taste for life that we otherwise almost forget we were created to cultivate in ourselves and in others. Another word for that particular conversion of delight effected by the Holy Spirit is "transformation" — not any transformation of any kind, but that radical change pointed to in Paul's second letter to the Corinthian congregation. "Now the Lord is the Spirit, and where the Spirit of the Lord is, there is freedom. And we all, with unveiled face, beholding the glory of the Lord, are being changed into his likeness from one degree of glory to another; for this comes from the Lord who is the Spirit. Therefore, having this ministry by the mercy of God, we do not lose heart" (2 Cor. 3:17–4:1).

We have noted the development of the doctrine of the Holy Spirit — the unfolding of what was contained, the making explicit of what was implicit. That applies to our personal development as members of the body of Christ. There is a rough but true correlation between (a) the historical development of the doctrine of the Holy Spirit and (b) the social and psychological development of our experience of the Holy Spirit. There is a rough but discernible correlation between the stages of human development and the stages of dawning realization of the work of the Holy Spirit in the life of a believer. It dawns on us more and more — sometimes colorfully and loudly, sometimes quietly and almost imperceptibly — that our growing freedom has been a gift of the Holy Spirit all along. This gift comes to us from beyond our best or worst capacities. The external words become God's Word to us — not just God's Word to others, but, *mirabile dictu,* God's Word to me a sinner who has never ceased to be divinely loved, a creature for whom God from all eternity has had a purpose.

The exact way that purpose unfolds differs from person to person, according to the widest panorama of social, economic, psychological, genetic, gender, chronological conditions imaginable. There is no doubt that for some people spiritual growth (growth in the Holy Spirit) entails ecstatic utterance: more power to them. Says Paul, in effect, in my colloquial paraphrase: "You want speaking in tongues? That I do. But being understood is more upbuilding of the body of Christ. That's what counts." (See the whole of 1 Corinthians 14.) There is no doubt that for some people spiritual growth entails the healing silence of quiet adoration. There is no doubt that for some people it entails being busy like Martha. For some, after the manner of Mary, it means meditation, slowing down to savor the presence while manifest. For everyone, I suppose, growth in the Spirit means all of the above, and more, in different combinations in different places and seasons.

The diversity with which members of the body of Christ experience the Holy Spirit constitutes the miraculous mutual enrichment of life together, what the old word "charity" used to mean. We are bound together in love, which is far more than liking or disliking one another. Christ commands us to love each other, which sometimes but not always includes even liking one another. Love means that we view with awe and encouraging liberality how others express their own developing experience of the work of the Holy Spirit in uniting us to Christ and to each other.

This Spirit-filled charity is one of the hardest things to maintain. It seems to be especially hard to maintain among those who are utterly confident that their brand of experience should be normative for everyone else. However, the Spirit is Lord, and that means that freeing love is the chief mark of the Spirit's presence:

freedom to hear in a practicing way the good news of God's reconciling presence and work in Jesus Christ. Rebirthing — being born again, regeneration — takes a wide range of struggles as believers cultivate and nourish their common life. A schismatic spirit is antithetical to the Holy Spirit, whose chief identifying mark is the upbuilding of the body of Christ. That is why among the three cardinal virtues, *love is the greatest:* that is, *faith-laden and hope-laden love.*

We noted above that theology is indeed "faith seeking understanding" *(fides quaerens intellectum),*[5] and that I choose to call sound theology even more *"love* seeking understanding" *(caritas quaerens intellectum).* This love also entails corrected, enlivening love of self in right relation to others. We will explore this realization more when we take up what it means to believe in the forgiveness of sins and the resurrection of the body. Here the main point is that the love that is the greatest of the virtues is *forward bent.* This love is alive with the vision of the peaceable kingdom, the holy mountain[6] of God's just peace. Love is the practice of compassion that counts on the ultimate triumph of God's benevolent purposes for all creation, including self. This kind of compassion treats other humans, and other creatures,[7] with the assumption that they are a precious part, an irreplaceable part, of that benevolent purpose of the Holy Triune. This is the kind of "rever-

---

5. Anselm, *Fides Quaerens Intellectum: id est, Proslogion . . .* (Paris: J. Vrin, 1992); Karl Barth, *Fides Quaerens Intellectum: Anselm's Proof . . .* (Richmond, Va.: John Knox, 1960); Daniel Migliore, *Faith Seeking Understanding: An Introduction to Christian Theology* (Grand Rapids Eerdmans, 1991).

6. Cf. the opening of chapter 8 on the future of forgiveness.

7. That includes the love for the environment for which we have a stewardship, an explication of which is nicely done in John Douglas Hall, *Steward* (Grand Rapids: Eerdmans, 1990). See also David Willis, "Proclaiming Liberation for the Earth's Sake," in *For Creation's Sake,* ed. Dieter T. Hessel (Philadelphia: Geneva Press, 1985), pp. 55-70.

ence for life" that is decisive, active, strategic, joyful, unsentimental, and always struggling over the practical priorities this reverence demands.

Before considering the intercessory office of the Spirit, we need to elucidate three consequences of the Spirit's sovereignty: first, the holy ordinariness of the Spirit's strategies; second, the special humility of those who realize they are born again; and third, the Pentecostal obedience of the faithful remnant.

The Holy Ordinariness of the Spirit

The *ordinariness* of the Spirit's presence and work belongs to the Spirit's *sovereignty*. There are doctrinal and ethical consequences to our believing in this sovereign ordinariness. By sovereignty in this context I mean the uncontrollable but utterly reliable power of the Spirit to effect the benevolent intentionality of God for his creation. By ordinariness I mean that which is local, tangible, workably predictable, menial, commonplace, mundane, concrete. By ordinariness I do not mean dull, colorless, banal, but their opposites. Recognizing the ordinary vividness, the revelatory hiddenness, of the Spirit's work is a guard against cloying sentimentality. The most commonly experienced fruit of the Spirit is often not recognized. I mean the moment-to-moment gift of enough power to persevere yet another day. I also mean the moment-to-moment gift with which the down-beaten and crushed cope with what is left of their lives and their loved ones' lives.

"Mundane" is a good word for the earthly and earthy work of the Holy Spirit. *Ordinarily the Holy Spirit works ordinarily.* That, after all, is the way of God toward the other — creation — he has intended into existence and continues to guide and sustain. Take the selling into bondage of Joseph whereby many were kept alive.

Take the stuttering of Moses, the one chosen to deliver the slaves from Egypt, and his helper Aaron. Take the sling and small stones against Goliath. Take from Mary's lips the Magnificat promise exalting the lowly and scattering the arrogant. Yes, take this Jewish maiden overshadowed by the Holy Spirit to bring forth Emmanuel. Take her son's obedience unto crucifixion. Take the humble origins of the apostolic community, the foolishness of God versus the wisdom of humans. And so on into the future.

So it is no surprise that the signs of the presence and labor of the Holy Spirit in our lives are usually confessed in retrospection. It is in healed memories, in turned-around consciousnesses, that we too say, "One thing I know, that though I was blind, now I see" (John 9:25). That was confessed by a person encountered and healed by Christ. But the same is true of the work of the Holy Spirit. The Holy Spirit did not begin to be present and active in our lives when we began to realize it. We began to realize it because the Holy Spirit had been working secretly, mundanely, ordinarily all our lives — and before, indeed, through the coming together of our own parents and gestation and labor and earliest nurture.

How can we say it more plainly? The Holy Spirit is not the human spirit writ large. The Holy Spirit is God who takes the material of our identity and transforms it. That includes the transformation that ordinarily takes place developmentally through successive stages of personality maturation. For some people this comes about dramatically, extraordinarily, unmistakably. However, for the vast majority of Christians, I dare say, it comes about through the cumulative energy of detailed authenticities.

This chief ordinary gift of the Spirit is the animating presence of the Spirit through all sorts and conditions of the tenuously human. I mean all those it is mortally easy to take for granted and to be taken for granted by. I mean the routine steadfastness of artists, painters, cancer patients and researchers, prison inmates and wardens, poets, street sweepers, nurses, social workers, carpenters, the homeless, diaper changers, farmers, those who struggle with their and others' addictions, lawyers, the jobless, politicians, pastors, teachers, pharmacologists, latrine cleaners, harbor pilots, tent builders, diplomats, soldiers, bureaucrats, deans, publishers, grade-schoolers, teenagers, athletes, tax collectors, mechanics — and their distant and near ilk.

I suppose part of what recommends the term "ordinariness" to me is that it is a guard against a misunderstanding of the supernatural. Acknowledging the ordinariness of the Spirit's work is a guard against the dreadful, and widespread, temptation to spiritualize the faith, to etherealize the Spirit, to gossamerize the concrete physicality of the Spirit's empowerment for service. The incarnation means that the God we know works through the natural to recover the natural. I am conscious of Bonhoeffer's helpful vocabulary on this point. When the knowledge of the Spirit takes root in the heart, we are compelled to confess that what is new is not so much the Spirit's work and presence. What is especially new is our discovery that the Spirit has been graciously, grittily, patiently, strategically, sometimes dramatically but often as not unobtrusively *at work all along,* unbeknownst to us, to bring us to this realization. There is a common phrase that goes "When the Holy Spirit came into my life . . ." What primarily is meant, I think, is "When the gospel awakened me to discern the work of the Spirit . . ." Or "When I became aware of my place in the life of the Spirit . . ."

The Special Humility of Those
Who Realize They Are Born Again

Sometimes "born-again Christians" (a redundant phrase) speak about their experiences in ways which are unnecessary stumbling blocks for other believers and for unbelievers. It is not that born-again Christians have not really been born again. They have. Rebirth is one of the canonical images recommended to us in the New Testament. It is, rather, that *some* persons who promote their identity as born-again Christians (a) speak and behave in ways which tend to call attention more to their own faith than to the one on whom faith is focused; (b) speak and behave as if their new life in Christ is relatively free of the highs and lows of struggling for authentic trust in the face of major challenges; and (c) speak and behave as if their being born again, with the marks they specify, makes them more Christian than others who have not had those defining experiences.

As a consequence, some ordinary Christians begin to doubt their own faithful struggles by comparing them to loud conversions. They think the piety of these born-again Christians is what everyone should achieve, whereas in fact, the New Testament treats one's piety as belonging more to authentic silence than to public manifestation. This was what Bonhoeffer was getting at with his recovering of the norm of the *secret discipline*.[8] In doing so, Bonhoeffer is just taking seriously what Christ says is characteristic of true, closeted, piety. The hypocrites (that's all of us in some way or another) pray in public to be seen and known as pious people. Hypocrites get what they want: they are noted for their piety. "But you . . . ," says Christ to the disciples. Disciples are to avoid appearances, performances, of piety. For their reward is to be seen not of humans but of the heavenly Father.

Notice that I have spoken of these people as those who realize they are born again. Their realization is not what sets them apart, nor is their realization a prerequisite for their personal renais-

---

8. See the treatment of the secret discipline in Dietrich Bonhoeffer, *The Cost of Discipleship* (New York: Macmillan, 1965), pp. 172-201, "Matthew Six: On the Hidden Character of the Christian Life."

sance. That is the point: they bring to their saving encounter with Christ, by the power of the Holy Spirit, no condition which would recommend them more than anyone else, including the condition of being more a sinner than others. Insisting on one's identity as having been the greatest sinner before conversion is a caustic form of pride. Notice that I say that those who know themselves to be born again (among whom everyone who takes the gospel to heart dares to count himself or herself) have a special calling to a special kind of humility. It is to a humility that is not noticed and is the opposite of thinking one is thereby spiritually superior, somehow a more advanced believer.

In fact, conversion is to a humility that is unaware of its humility. I think, for example, of the main character in Georges Bernanos's *Diary of a Country Priest,*[9] whose authenticity includes his being unaware of his humility and who takes all the risks of loving the troubled which his more successful colleague priest in the next village does not take. Or I think of the whiskey priest in Graham Greene's *The Power and the Glory.*[10] There is something almost self-contradictory in naming this or that person a saint because of something dramatic he or she did. Anonymity of self-giving love is usually one of the most important aspects of the Christian life. The vast majority of holy ones who do selfless (and therefore self-discovering) deeds of love are not remembered except by our Father who sees and rewards. Now there is indeed specialness of being born again, secret though it normally is. As we noted above, the very name of the church *(ekklesia)* means to be called out, set apart for service. Service means the hyphenated reality worship-witness-caring. Here we need only reemphasize

9. Georges Bernanos, *Diary of a Country Priest* (New York: Macmillan, 1937).

10. Graham Greene, *The Power and the Glory* (New York: Viking Press, 1990). I find that mainly to be the case with Hazel Motes in Flannery O'Connor's *Wise Blood:* Flannery O'Connor, *Three: "Wise Blood," "A Good Man Is Hard to Find," "The Violent Bear It Away"* (New York: New American Library, 1962).

that that specialness of service is the kind that does not call attention to itself.

The Pentecostal Obedience of the Faithful Remnant

Pentecost has undergone a severe privatization. By privatization I mean making Pentecost as described in Acts a particularly moving example of what supposedly really counts, namely, an individual's personal experience of the Holy Spirit. This privatization forgets that the individual Christian's truest self is her or his co-membership in the body of Christ. It ignores the fact that we find ourselves by stepping into that great procession of holy ones stretching way back and way forward. I think here of Mrs. Turpin's vision in Flannery O'Connor's "Revelation." Again, I think of the saints facing forward in the mosaics in St. Apollinare-in-Classe, Ravenna.

The communal setting of Pentecost is so evident that we need not devote much attention to the danger of privatization. We can, rather, focus on the glory of the new development taking place with faithful Israel on that day. The glory of Pentecost has mainly — not only, but mainly — to do with two things.

First, Pentecost has to do with the fulfillment of the prophets' vision and message. The phrase in the Nicene Creed, "Who spoke by the prophets," refers to the Holy Spirit. The irreducible core of the earliest apostolic proclamation is that what has happened with the coming, death, and resurrection of Jesus is the fulfillment of the promises made to Israel through the prophets. Here we have the reading for the second Sunday after Easter (Acts 3:12a, 13-15, 17-26):

> When Peter saw [the people running toward John and him] he addressed the people, "Men of Israel, . . . the God of

Abraham and of Isaac and of Jacob, the God of our fathers, glorified his servant Jesus, whom you delivered up and denied in the presence of Pilate, when he had decided to release him. But you denied the Holy and Righteous One, and asked for a murderer to be granted to you, and killed the Author of life, whom God raised from the dead. To this we are witnesses. . . . And now, brethren, I know that you acted in ignorance, as did also your rulers. But what God foretold by the mouth of all the prophets, that his Christ should suffer, he thus fulfilled. Repent therefore, and turn again, that your sins may be blotted out, that times of refreshing may come from the presence of the Lord, and that he may send the Christ appointed for you, Jesus, whom heaven must receive until the time for establishing all that God spoke by the mouth of his holy prophets from of old. Moses said, 'The Lord God will raise up for you a prophet from your brethren as he raised me up. You shall listen to him in whatever he tells you. And it shall be that every soul that does not listen to that prophet shall be destroyed from the people.' And all the prophets who have spoken, from Samuel and those who came afterwards, also proclaimed these days. You are the sons of the prophets and of the covenant which God gave to your fathers, saying to Abraham, 'And in your posterity shall all the families of the earth be blessed.' God, having raised up his servant, sent him to you first, to bless you in turning every one of you from your wickedness."

The critical point is that with the death and resurrection of Jesus the Christ, the long-awaited deliverance of Israel is at hand, but a deliverance that caught — and *catches* — every one of the disciples by sacred surprise. A dreadful mistake, as far as human standards of justice are concerned, has been made. An innocent man

— *the* innocent one — has been executed by the cruelest means Rome had of keeping Rome's enemies in line. Peter's proclamation exposed the deepest, unbearable crisis facing Israel — and facing us time and time again. There was no room, there *is* no room, to hide or pretend or rationalize. Their — *our* — part in the Messiah's crucifixion was — *is* — inescapable. The question is crushed out of them — out of *us:* "What must *we* do to be saved?" The answer is startling, focused, as urgent as the question: "Turn completely around [repent], believe the good news, and be baptized."

Baptism is an act of repentance. Baptism is not a coming-out party for adults or for children. It has nothing to do with the innocence and indisputable cuteness of babies, grown-up or otherwise. Baptism has to do with being convicted of sin and being driven to seek to be saved. Oh, there are other things thrown in, other social conventions that are delightful in their own ways. But baptism has centrally to do with being united by the Spirit to the one whose cross we also thereby own and covenant to follow wherever discipleship leads us. The remission of sin for which there is one baptism, is above all for the sin of the betrayal of Jesus the Christ. Ultimately included in this betrayal are the myriad other ways we have of refusing God's sovereign love. Betrayal implies knowing better; it implies being a member of some trusting circle; it implies turning one's back on someone who has benefited one. The greater the benefactor's trust, the greater the betrayal. That is what those gathered from all over at Jerusalem realized that day. That is fundamentally the condition to which being baptized is a response.

Saints — those made holy by the Holy Spirit — are not created out of nothing. Saints are created out of sinner material. Sinners are the ones Christ came into the world to save. That's us, the motley stumblers, the wayward offending, the pigheaded hungry, the willfully ignorant. Sinners are changed, not disposed of. Pentecost is about new beginnings of old lives. As Paul would cry, "I, yet not I, but Christ in me." Pentecostal experience is a paradigm for subsequent experiences of the Spirit's work. The Spirit's work is to give life through radical discontinuity and restoration of continuity at a new level of freedom and justice. The change is often gentle, but for all its gentleness it is radical. It entails unveiling where there was deceit, healing where there was sickness unto death, miraculous hope where there was grinding despair, compassionate understanding where there was sadistic blaming, life together where there was isolation, good conscience where there was bad, joy in serving others where there was tedious self-absorption, and so on.

A malpractice has crept into some lately popular religion: the practice of calling Pentecost the "birthday of the church" and the cutesy stickiness of passing out cupcakes with a candle. Oh, I know it is a catchy device intended to call attention to the importance of Pentecost as a great and joyous feast day, but it minimizes — even ignores — the continuity of the church in the Old and New Testaments. One can, of course, by definition mean by church that fellowship which succeeds Israel, but that is a dangerous use of words. It forgets the fact that the new covenant is a fulfillment of the old. This malpractice forgets chapters 11 and 12 of Hebrews. As an antidote to this poisonous malpractice, take the wonderful definition of the church in the Scots Confession: the Kirk is the communion of the faithful in all times and places, moving from Adam and Eve forward, including all those who in eternity sing God's praises.

Outstanding among the faithful in all times and places is Mary. Here is a laughably understated truth: Mary has a special place in the unfolding of God's gracious strategy. In replying to the angel Gabriel's message, she says, "Let it be to me according to thy word." That response defines free obedience for all of us, a particular kind of obedience that is incumbent upon all to whom the Word is freshly addressed by successive messengers.

If there were a most unpopular word today, it would be, I think, "obedience." There is a good reason for rejecting some calls to obedience. For too long and in too many cultures obedience meant shutting up and doing what you were told by those in authority over you — whether or not the authorities knew what in the world they were doing. By contrast, the obedience that is an inevitable ingredient of Christian discipleship is of a different order. "Obedience" here is not primarily a character trait or a virtue or — for sure — pliant acquiescence. Obedience is not finally giving in to tiresome nagging or threatened violence. It is not what you do at the expense of loss of will.

Obedience — if we are to judge from Mary's response — is an active, busy, robust, courageous decision to hear and do what we imperfectly but sufficiently identify as God's Word to us. That Word is not any old or any new word. God's Word is not fashionable palaver. It is surely not verbiage we can become skilled at packaging, adept at rendering relevant, professional at hawking for a price. The Word cannot be made into utilitarian religion. It is not automatically accessible. The false prophets claim they always have a word from the Lord. The true prophets wait long periods when there seems to be no Word from God. What else is faith than the waiting time and again for the Word because the Word commands us to do so? The Word of God comes to us from the depth of God's love, freedom, power. It comes to us when and where God wills it, and it comes to us where we are. The Word is historically mediated, or it is not our God's Word.

The Word comes to us through different messengers at different times in different contexts — as we shall see when we speak about the church's being one, holy, catholic, and apostolic. Trusting the Holy Spirit means trusting that the written Word will guide us, in the context of the believing community and with the community's help, to hear and do the next thing God may have in store for us. Such obedience is not evoked by threatened evil but by delight in the one whom the obeying one most loves. "Let it be to me according to thy Word." This is what Mary says back to the angel, and this is the response Christians struggle to practice all their lives and in every corner of their lives.[11]

The glory of Pentecost has, secondly, to do with *the universality of the gospel.* Those at Pentecost appeared to be drunk — but it was still too early in the day for that! The symptoms turned out to be an explosion of tongues being spoken — *and understood* — by Jews from all over the whole inhabited earth. The word for "whole inhabited earth" is behind the word "ecumenical." That is a clue to an important fact about the growth of the Christian community. Universality means in the first instance the *earthly location* of the believing community. The believing community is every*where;* it shows up in every *place* where people gather. The church exists on earth, called by the Word in the world to be about earthly mission. Oh, indeed the church *also* exists in heaven, but the contours of the whole company of heaven, including the angels and archangels and what they do, are not what concern us now.

What concerns us now is the earthly outcropping of that company which has come before us and will come after us, the beloved, earthy, struggling, victorious, puzzled and puzzling pilgrims, the band of forgiven sinners, the advanced guard of the society God wills for all his people. Pentecost has to do with the reversal of the curse upon tongues at Babel. After the tower of Babel, no matter how clearly people spoke in their own currency, persons were tragically given to misunderstanding. Diverse

11. That is what the Barmen Declaration is also getting at. There are no areas where the freely given justification and sanctification of Christ do not apply. In every area, in life and in death, there is one Word whom we hear, trust, and obey: Jesus Christ as attested in the Scriptures of the Old and New Testaments. (The First Evangelical Truth, Barmen Declaration, Presbyterian Church U.S.A., *The Constitution, Part I, Book of Confessions* [Louisville: Office of the General Assembly, 1994].)

tongues often functioned not as vehicles of understanding but as barriers. Pentecost means that is changed. The capacity to understand, the remarkable discovery that we understand and are understood, is paramount at Pentecost. This is one of the chief works of the Holy Spirit, one of the chief marks of the Spirit's presence: that we speak out of who we are and in our terms, and others do the same, and, *mirabile dictu* — we actually understand one another more and more. With that comes incredible, undreamt-of assurance and joy.

Humans are created linguistic creatures. One of the most primordial human hungers is to express and receive expression, to evoke and to respond. The joy of restored understanding is indescribable. The hunger to communicate is one of the needs that God hears and responds to, just as he heard the cries of his people in bondage and did something about it to deliver them. This need to hear and be heard in some form or another applies also — no, perhaps especially — to the mentally ill, to the mute, to the stammering, to the palsied, to the deaf. Their confusion, despair, pain, frustration, maddening dumbness and deafness are not to be minimized or sentimentalized. But Pentecost does mean that their belonging to the community, their contribution, is essential to the wholeness of the community's hearing and doing; and it means ingenuity and action, including skilled technicians, to encourage their share in the commonweal.

We tend most to think of the function of the Holy Spirit abetting speaking the Word and hearing the Word, and we do so because that is the way of perhaps most of Scripture. But the "Word" of God is, as we noted in chapter 4 on the incarnation, much, much larger than just the articulated, voiced Word, and much larger than its written, canonical form. This means at least two things.

First, it means that we have to recognize the importance of *the body language of the church.* I mean the sacred actions, for example of breaking bread and pouring wine, of pouring running water, of exchanging the peace among members of the congregation, and so on. Some will want to include vestments, kneeling, making the sign of the cross, processing, and so on in this category. It is inaccurate to refer to these actions as "nonverbal communication." The body language of the church is not "nonverbal." It is another way of enhancing and reinforcing the spoken and read word. It is a way of being most profoundly verbal, a way the Word takes root in the heart. The vocabulary, as it were, of the church's body language is a means by which the Word is accommodated to people's social, economic, political, psychological, physical conditions. The Holy Spirit takes the things of Christ and applies them to us. Part of the way the Holy Spirit does that work is through the nonvocal but profoundly verbal body language of the liturgy.

Second, the *para-vocal work of the Holy Spirit* means that silence is often the richest form of the Word. Those who cannot speak and cannot hear are often far more eloquent messengers of the word than the habitually loquacious. As often as not, the Holy Spirit moves us to silence. Growth in the Spirit often as not means the practice of not speaking. By the power of the Spirit, the Word often calls us to the active discipline of keeping still. One of the main ways the body of Christ is upbuilt is through loving silence. "Whatever happened to sin?" Karl Menninger asked.[12] Well, whatever happened to prudence? Whatever happened to that tact, pastoral sensibility, civility that takes more delight in another's goodness than in repeating tales of another's faults? There is a great deal of wisdom in the folk adage that says if you cannot say something kind about a person, don't say anything.

At least we know that the commandment against bearing false witness includes the prohibition of gossip. Idle talk, gossip,

---

12. Karl Menninger, *Whatever Happened to Sin?* (New York: Hawthorne, 1973).

about another person is also a violation of the commandment not to kill. On the positive side, often as not, compassionate silence — intelligent listening — is the truest, most accurate, most candid way of sharing another person's joy or pain. We say we are "struck speechless" by this or that event, person, art — and so it is. We are quite literally struck dumb by the beauty of this or that — or by appalling cruelty. Dumbness is often the truest response to the magnitude of what encounters us. That is quite the opposite of thinking that something is real to the extent that we can control it by our chatter.

I have come across some interpretations of Pentecost that see in it the phenomenon of glossolalia, so called "speaking in tongues." As we noted above, Paul is pretty clear,[13] it seems to me, that tonguing is both an approved phenomenon — ecstatic utterance — and a gift that has to be used with great care lest it become a hindrance to understanding. Paul claims that if you want ecstatic utterance, he can give you that too; but what really counts is intelligible communication, clear intercourse, accurate parlance — and that is the *gift of prophecy.* "The gift of prophecy" is a daring term for Paul to use. It means being moved by the Holy Spirit to speak the Word of God, and is conferred often as not on one who had not planned on speaking it. The term is daring, for it connotes the experience of those to whom the Word of the Lord came with such power and bite that they could not remain silent in the face of Israel's forgetting to whom she belongs.

Here is Paul, applying that term "prophecy,"[14] reserved for a high office in God's dealing with Israel, to a gift given to some in the Christian community to hear and speak God's Word. Paul is thereby defining the prophetic gift as that which makes clear

13. Cf. 1 Cor. 14:1-33.
14. See Thomas W. Gillespie, *The First Theologians: A Study in Early Christian Prophecy* (Grand Rapids: Eerdmans, 1994).

("elucidates": lets there be light) what God is saying to humanity in the Word made flesh and enabling humanity to respond to him and to each other. In short, the gift of prophecy is communication that details God's universal love. The gift of prophecy facilitates the speaking and hearing of the gospel to and from each other. Paul puts the matter forcefully:

> Make love your aim, and earnestly desire the spiritual gifts, especially that you may prophesy. For one who speaks in a tongue speaks not to men but to God; for no one understands him, but he utters mysteries in the Spirit. On the other hand, he who prophesies speaks to men for their upbuilding and encouragement and consolation. He who speaks in a tongue edifies himself, but he who prophesies edifies the church. Now I want you all to speak in tongues, but even more to prophesy. He who prophesies is greater than he who speaks in tongues, unless someone interprets, so that the church may be edified. (1 Cor. 14:1-5)

The Intercessory Office of the Holy Spirit

According to Romans 8, the Holy Spirit prays on our behalf when we know not how. This office is another mercy of the Spirit's sovereignty. Above I argued that the individual believer's very own identity is his or her co-membership in the body of Christ. In that life together we discover a greater and freer individuality than we would were we to keep scratching about for our own personal identity, believer or not. Now I am compelled to extend the implications of the Spirit's being not just the Spirit who effects redemption of humans but the Spirit who sustains the whole world as it undergoes the travail, the birth pangs, of a new future for all the earth.

This is where God's redeeming work and God's creating work

are shown ultimately to be two sides of the same coin. Redemption is not primarily deliverance from the world, escape into a realm above, untouched by the fluctuations and anguishes and passing joys and unbearable pains and injustices and defeats and fragilities that beset all humans, believers or not, in differing timings and degrees. As we noted earlier, redemption is not primarily deliverance from something. We are delivered from, yes — but we are delivered by being included in a sovereignly graceful reality. *Redemption is primarily ultimate inclusion in the shalom of God* — inclusion in the finally triumphant justice, the finally loving festive peace God brought his creation into being in the first place to enjoy. "And all shall be well and all manner of thing shall be well." "And we shall all be welcome under the wide wishing tree." "And all shall come, from east and from west, and sit at table together." "And none shall kill in all my holy mountain." And so on.

If we define redemption only as deliverance from something — salvation only as not going to hell, say — then we have already yielded the high ground to evil and let it define what we mean by good. When we do that, in other words, we have turned Augustine's definition of evil (the *privatio boni*) on its head and made (cross yourself here) evil the rule and not the rebellious exception, and defined good as the absence of evil! Yes, indeed and of course, evil has a derivative reality. Though derivative, evil has a reality so graphic and insidious and enormously attractive and therefore all the more destructive that we dare not think we can take it on by our own cleverness and piety. That is what baptism is all about: the confessing act by which we are ratified as belonging not to sin, death, and the devil, but to Jesus Christ, who has experienced the depth of everything evil could muster and has sprung the gates of hell and risen in triumph, the firstfruits of those who are joined to him in his death and so also joined to him in his resurrection. I know that is a mouthful, but sometimes the whole interconnectedness of victory needs to be sung in one long measure.

When we cannot pray as we ought, for any of a vast range of reasons, then the Spirit intercedes for us with groaning too deep for utterance. That means that technically we never fall out of the praying society of the Holy Spirit. In the deepest trough of our anger, sense of injustice, bitterness, apathy, suicidal trials and suicidal accomplishments — in even these personal forms of creation's groaning and much more — God himself, the Holy Spirit, intercedes in our stead. We have seen the sense in which Christ's redemptive work is standing in for us in fulfillment of the covenant. A parallel vicariousness is the Holy Spirit's intercession when we cannot intercede ourselves. In fact, Christ the risen Lord never ceases to intercede for us. For the Holy Spirit and the Eternal Word can never be separated. Where we have the activity and presence of one, we have the activity and presence of the other.

The Spirit intercedes for us. Goodness knows we need intercession. However, we are called to intercede for others. Moreover, our intercessions are also for the rest of creation. Our crying to God for selves and others is part of creation's groaning. The shalom toward which the whole of creation is moving includes care for the rest of creation besides humanity. There is no shalom where the rest of creation and humanity are not in right relationship. There is no shalom when the dichotomy prevails of user and used, of exploiter and exploited, of corrupter and corrupted. The tension and the ultimate hope are well expressed in Gerard Manley Hopkins's poem that we cited above.

Now I need to have a word with and for Ivan Karamazov.[15] He is a holy man in his refusal of cheaply offered answers. He is a flesh and blood saint in his refusal to romanticize or diminish the facts that while God seems theoretically in charge of benevolent purposes, nothing can ever make up for the injustice and unimaginable cruelty of the dogs being sicced on the peasant children.

---

15. Fyodor Dostoevsky, *The Brothers Karamazov* (New York: Norton, 1976).

Even if that were the only absurdly cruel action (which it is not), the question would still be, how can one believe in God's sovereign goodness in the face of such injustice and suffering? Just to say it all belongs to creation's groaning is not enough, true though it may be.

I am not aware of any convincing answer to Ivan's question — but more power to those who wrestle with the angel to offer one. Ivan's question is everyone's — expressed or not, realized or not. Woe to those who think we have an easy answer to that question. And woe upon woe to those who try to offer comforting words when there is no comfort, who whisper "Peace, peace" where there is no peace. The only modicum of comfort consists in the presence of loved ones in bereavement — and in action to correct as much as possible (many times it is not possible) the conditions behind such tragedy. The only thing which makes sense when there is no sense to be made, is the honesty to confess that while the whole of creation is moving toward the inclusive shalom, we are far from that culmination and there are often precious few signs of that movement.

This realism is the opposite of a counsel of despair. The latter copes with tragedy by elaborate forms of denial, by whistling in the dark, by grinning surface jocularity that masks deep labyrinthine melancholy. Becoming arrested at one stage of grieving is also a way of exhibiting nostalgia for conditions before the tragedy. By sharpest contrast to wishful fantasy that minimizes tragedy, and as contrast to the manipulative refusal to be consoled, is the way of the cross. The way of the cross is not a formula that closes off argument. It is a sign once again that the God we trust is the one who goes to the far country to take on our condition, tragedy and all. Whatever else can be said, this is true: God himself has entered into our own predicament and possibility, and his descent and rising mean there is no place we can be where he has not already been before and after us.

The whole wide earth, not just humanity, groans toward its deliverance into God's shalom. The only comfort is that of co-belonging with the rest of God's creation, of being part of that unfolding expanding universe which is going no one knows where. For Christians there is content to this belonging; there is focus by which this universal belonging is identified. The content and focus are what we are reminded of by the first question of the Heidelberg Catechism, which I, by conviction and for reasons given above, dare emend in brackets. "What is your only comfort in life and in death?" "That I [and my loved ones, and my enemies, and ultimately the whole of creation] belong body and soul, in life and in death, not to myself [ourselves] but to my [our] faithful Savior Jesus Christ who at the cost of his own blood has fully paid for all my [our] sins."[16]

Procession and Mission

There remains in this chapter to note one of the most debated wordings in the Nicene Creed: what it means to say that the Spirit "proceeds from the Father" or "proceeds from the Father and the Son." There are issues at stake in both versions, but here our main concern is to point to what the term "procession" means with regard to the Holy Spirit in either case.

To do so, we need to bring forward and apply what we said above about the analogical character of creedal language: to what our human thinking and speaking are referring when we use of God the words "Father" and "Creator" and "Son" and "Eternally Begotten" and "Light of Light." The term "Spirit" is already an analogical sign. The Hebrew word *ruach*, the Greek *pneuma*, the Latin *Spiritus* mean, with different nuances, moving air, wind,

---

16. Presbyterian Church U.S.A., *Book of Confessions*, p. 29.

breath. Each of those connotations is important to the power of the term "Spirit." Air usually is not directly visible, only in its effects or only when loaded with some material that makes the currents apparent. Wind is most likely to mean strongly moving air, that which displaces: a moving force to be dealt with — as nomads and sailors are especially likely to know. There are several words (like *nephesh* and *animus*) used for breath: the air inhaled and exhaled and inhaled to make a living being out of some thing.

"Procession" is a similarly multilayered word, a laminated expression. The latter word — "expression" — is pretty close to one of the main things connoted by "procession." Eternal glory moving, effulgent love communing, deepest-down mystery self-giving, pure simplicity outbursting, timeless joy forthgoing — all these images point to the ineluctable reality who is the Spirit, dynamic being prior to the creature's existence, awe, adoration. The Holy Spirit cannot be reduced to being "the subjective principle in religion." The Spirit's work is simultaneously inner and outer, subjective and objective (neither one without the other, as Vuillard and the other syncretists knew so well),[17] personal and cosmic. In each of these dimensions the Spirit is the dynamic going forth, the efficacious presence, of God's loving to be for another. God loves to be for another. The worldly mission of the church is grounded in the dynamic of God's own going forth, God's own mission.

This holy dynamism is counter to all that is stagnant, static, septic. This dynamism is effectively pointed to in the fecund overshadowing of Mary, in the anointed one's baptism, in Christ's miracles and teaching and passionate obedience, in the resurrection of the crucified one, in the going forth of the apostles from one culture into the whole inhabited earth, in the waiting with lamps

17. Guy Cogeval, *Vuillard: Post-Impressionist Master* (New York: Abrams, 2002).

trimmed for the one who is coming again, in the repentance and new beginnings of those who in each era and moment are moved into the range of the good news — in short, in the manner of the Spirit's going forth to unite believers to Christ and to each other in his body. Speaking in tongues and making tonguing intelligible are indeed evocative forms of the body language of the church. Perhaps even more so, though, is the epiclesis of the Holy Spirit upon the elements of bread and wine and upon the congregation. So is the procession behind the cross, the pacing selves behind Christ, putting one foot in front of another in daily discipleship. The people of God gather for the service of God in worship and go forth for the worship of God in service. Such holy going hither and yon smacks of life being poured out and poured forth in love. Such power enabling new beginnings, such going forwardly, indeed points, however so remotely, to the mystery of God eternally proceeding.

CHAPTER SEVEN

The Mystical Body

✠ ✠

Here is what our ordinary congregation ordinarily prays after receiving Communion:

> Almighty and everliving God, we most heartily thank thee for that thou dost feed us, in these holy mysteries, with the spiritual food of the most precious Body and Blood of thy Son our Savior Jesus Christ; and dost assure us thereby of thy favor and goodness towards us; and that we are very members incorporate in the mystical body of thy Son, the blessed company of all faithful people; and are heirs, through hope, of thy everlasting kingdom. And we humbly beseech thee, O heavenly Father, so to assist us with thy grace, that we may continue in that holy fellowship, and do all such good works as thou hast prepared for us to walk in; through Jesus Christ our Lord, to whom, with thee and the Holy Spirit, be all honor and glory, world without end. Amen.[1]

1. The Episcopal Church, *The Book of Common Prayer* (New York: Church Hymnal Corporation and Seabury Press, 1977), p. 339.

This language takes us to the heart of the mystery of Christ's uniting us to himself. For centuries this union of Christ with the church has been spoken of in the terms lavishly and daringly provided by the Song of Songs.[2] That is because apparently the closest thing we have in human experience of the love of Christ for the church is that of a person deeply in love with another person and willing and eager to make the costly decisions and actions such love inspires. We have come to use the word "inspires" loosely, but in this context it means quite specifically the fact, power, presence, action of the Holy Spirit in uniting us to Christ and to each other — and in reuniting self to self, the reintegration of our truest being.

---

2. Recall Bonhoeffer's comment, in his letter of May 20, 1944, from Tegel, to Bethge, about the good news that Song of Songs is part of the canon. It is one of the most important passages in Bonhoeffer's writings: "God wants us to love him eternally with our whole hearts — not in such a way as to injure or weaken our earthly love, but to provide a kind of *cantus firmus* to which the other melodies of life provide the counterpoint. One of these contrapuntal themes (which have their own complete independence but are yet related to the *cantus firmus*) is earthly affection. Even in the Bible we have the Song of Songs; and really one can imagine no more ardent, passionate, sensual love than is portrayed there (see 7.6). It's a good thing the book is in the Bible, in face of all those who believe that the restraint of passion is Christian (where is there such restraint in the Old Testament?). Where the *cantus firmus* is clear and plain, the counterpart can be developed to its limits. The two are 'undivided yet distinct,' in the words of the Chalcedonian Definition, like Christ in his divine and human natures. May not the attraction and importance of polyphony in music consist in its being a musical reflection of this Christological fact and therefore of our *vita christiana*? . . . Only a polyphony of this kind can give life a wholeness and at the same time assure us that nothing calamitous can happen as long as the *cantus firmus* is kept going." Dietrich Bonhoeffer, *Letters and Papers from Prison,* enlarged edition by Eberhard Bethge (New York: Macmillan, 1972), p. 303.

Recovering Prophetic Mysticism

The uniting office of the Holy Spirit is exactly what is meant in this context by the term "mystic." It is a shame we have let that term fall into abuse or disuse. "Mystical" is a strong word which is too rich to be left to its despisers who think it means the opposite of prophetic. It does not mean escape from the world, impersonal absorption into infinite vagueness. On the contrary, almost all the great leaders of the church have belonged to a broadly defined mystical tradition.[3] Each of these leaders gave much attention to the individual's relation to Christ. How could they not, if they read the New Testament accounts of Christ's dealing with persons in their own particularity? But invariably for these mystics, the union with Christ was the result of, and the direction of, union with other believers. The union with Christ is — to use Edwards's phrase — a *society of divine happiness.* The social content to mysticism is what is going on when Calvin writes the fourth book of the *Institutes,* by far the largest of those books, on the church and calls it the Society of Christ. Calvin is not particularly unusual in this usage, though the corporate character of union with Christ is put in numerous ways by other thinkers.

3. Paul gave it its initial direction and momentum. Believers — not just theologians and monks but all the apostolate — in what came to be Eastern Orthodoxy, particularly enhanced it. It was, however, no less present in Western spirituality than in the East. Just think of Augustine and his many shades of followers. It is outstanding in such great figures as Hugh of St. Victor, Aquinas, Bonaventura, Catherine of Siena, St. John of the Cross, Teresa of Avila, Luther, Calvin — to say nothing of the Zinzendorfians and those they spawned, including Bonhoeffer. Take Bernard of Clairvaux. He was hardly uninvolved in the great political, social, cultural upheavals of his time. We may well disagree with much of his political direction, but we have to acknowledge that his mysticism was a condition of his engagement. The same is true of the major reformer who drew so heavily on Bernard, Calvin. Cf. Anthony Lane, *Calvin and Bernard of Clairvaux* (Princeton: Princeton Theological Seminary, 1996).

Of course, if the terms used in the mystical tradition are a stumbling block to weaker brothers and sisters, then one must be free to use other language. What counts is not the term "mystical" or "mystic" but the matter, however it is referred to. That matter is not a thing of indifference. It is essential to the Christian faith. I mean the fact that Christ ties, binds, unites us to himself and to other believers in his body, the church. The church is a human, sociologically examinable, mixed company. Each person therein is himself or herself a hodgepodge of mixed motives, unfinished agendas, shadow sides, stages of development. The body is pied beauty, a collection of mutterers of the Mass and sonorous callers to repentance.

The church is all that — but it is more. It is indeed all that, but it is also a miracle. It is a miracle in the strict sense of miracle: an effective sign of the presence of the kingdom ushered in by Jesus the Christ and the fresh outpouring of the Holy Spirit on not just Israel but on people of all nations and ages. That beyondness — that "more than" — is the presence and activity of Christ who is the life of which their life together is an expression. This presence is what sustains the church's hope: the trust that God will never cease to use the earthen vessels to convey the gospel.[4] The church is like a bride in the sense that she is pledged to one and still awaits the final consummation with Christ's return. Because Christ is the groom, the church lives from moment to moment by this hope and itself is a hope-engendering, freeing community because it is the community that struggles by grace to live by grace.

4. Cf. Avery Dulles, *Models of the Church,* expanded edition (New York: Doubleday, Image Books, 1987); James M. Gustafson, *Treasure in Earthen Vessels: The Church as a Human Community* (New York: Harper, 1961); Dietrich Bonhoeffer, *The Communion of Saints* (New York: Harper and Row, 1963); Clifford J. Green, *Bonhoeffer: A Theology of Sociality* (Grand Rapids: Eerdmans, 1999); and the still relevant Frederick W. Dillistone, *The Structure of the Divine Society* (London: Lutterworth, 1951).

There is a teaching that is not to be confused with recognizing the church to be the mystical body of Christ. I mean the *idealization* of the church. By that I mean the view that the true church is an ideal church. On the contrary, the mystical body of Christ[5] is the visible, tangible, fragmented, ambiguity-laden, struggling, dubiously faithful congregation of forgiven sinners that lives day in and day out by the power of the Word and Spirit. The mystical body is not restricted to its earthly, earthy manifestation at any one time or in one culture. The reality of which it is a part extends beyond the presently visible church and includes "all the company of heaven."

The whole company of heaven is vastly larger and more diverse than any single earthly expression of it. This realization is a source of immense comfort and strength to those who are being tested almost beyond their endurance. Every time we say the "Amen" to the Lord's Prayer we remind ourselves — so Luther puts it — that we belong to the multitudes of other times and places who are joined in saying this prayer. We remind ourselves that we belong to the fellowship of all the company of heaven, together with the proximate fellowship of earthly members. We do not have direct access to the whole company of heaven. We share in the *communio sanctorum* only by being a part of the motley fellowship of those who, from the beginning, did not choose Christ but were chosen by him.

The "according to the Word of God reforming and always to be reformed church" is the true church of whatever denomination.[6] The continuity of prophetic reform belongs to the very nature of the church's catholicity. The church does not begin to be

5. Dulles, *Models of the Church,* chap. 3: "The Church as Mystical Communion." See also John Meyendorf, *Catholicity and the Church* (Crestwood, N.Y.: St. Vladimir's Seminary Press, 1983), chap. 1: "The Theology of the Holy Spirit."

6. John Hesselink, *On Being Reformed* (New York: Reformed Church Press, 1988).

the church when it has achieved some self-set goal or agreed-upon mission statement. It is in its pilgrimage as the people of God, living by the daily bread of the Word, that the church is the mystical body of Christ.

Five Complementarities of the True Church

We have already said something about the fact that the revealed and the hidden forms of reality are inseparable. Hiddenness-revealedness is a hyphenated reality. The revealed God is the hidden God and the hidden God is the revealed God, though hiddenness is deeper than revealedness. The implications of this are important for our understanding of the nature of the church as the mystical body of Christ.

We shall presently say something about the four most-mentioned marks of the true church. Before that, though, we need to be alert to five *poles of tensions* which constitute the very humanity and very glory of that community which Christ unites to himself by the bond of the Spirit. Those five poles are: *elect and rejected, already and not yet, visible and invisible, spotless and sinful, triumphant and militant.* Each pole applies to the mystical body of Christ. Each pole is a dialectical reality instead of a complex of opposites. All five pairs (or poles) are efforts to answer the question, *What is the true church?* That question implies that there is a true church; that there is such a thing as truth which is a characteristic of a community; and that the question is serious because not every part of the life of the community that names itself after Jesus Christ exhibits the fruits of the faith it professes.

Put otherwise, these poles belong to the very nature of being a prophetic community. A prophetic community hears the Word that comes by the prophets, and in turn calls out a prophetic word. The community's own weaknesses are so manifest that it must continually reaffirm its solidarity with those who make no pretense to spiritual depth or social righteousness. The church is an instrument — although not the only one — through which Christ is exercising his offices of prophet, priest, and king. It exercises a prophetic function in hearing and speaking a prophetic word, a priestly office when it intercedes on behalf of the downtrodden, and a royal office when it engages in the politics of the proximity of the kingdom of God. In these ways the church's life mirrors the offices by which Christ is the one sufficient Mediator.[7] The prophetic office, however, is the chief one; it orders the others because the community remains in sane trajectory as long as, and only insofar as, it hears and trusts and obeys the Word of God freshly coming to it.

The church elect and rejected and *the church already and not yet* are presuppositional for the other three poles. The *elect-rejected* pair and the *already–not yet* pair inform the right understanding of the other pairs. I mean that they are what lies behind other descriptions of the church, and they pose the questions other expressions must account for. Israel experiences being called by this God and thereby becoming this particular people. Believers in Jesus the Christ experience being called to follow him with others who thereby share a common identity. The complementarities of *elect and rejected* and *already and not yet* are inevitable poles in the definition of the church as the mystical body of Christ. The church is — by being united to Christ by the bond of the Holy Spirit — the elect *and* rejected company which already is, and yet not fully is, the communion of holy ones.[8] Perfection is already tasted — as

---

7. Note that I have deliberatively specified the only *sufficient* Mediator, for there are arrays of penultimate, derivative mediator figures, none of which is the singularly full and sufficient Mediator.

8. Cf. Pierre Maury, *Predestination . . . with Foreword by Karl Barth* (Richmond, Va.: John Knox, 1960), and Karl Barth, "The Election of God," in *Church Dogmatics* I/1–IV/4 (Edinburgh: T. & T. Clark, 1936-69), II/2, par. 32-35.

something only experienced now as a promise, but thereby not less real. Both rejection and election, in reverse order of magnitude and duration, are experiential givens by which we know we are known and freely, utterly graciously, accepted by Christ. That identity is the communion of ones holy in Christ from before the foundation of the world.

The Church Visible and Invisible

It was Albrecht Ritschl, I believe, who is supposed to have said that the pietist Arnold sought to write a history of the invisible church. That was not entirely fair to Arnold and Francke and their ilk. The point, however, that Ritschl was making is valid: the true church is not some ideal unobservable in this world. Being the church is living rightly in this world and in these times, and that means struggling from culture to culture to approximate what the Word compels us to mean by rightly living.

When Calvin speaks of the invisible church, he does not mean a community we cannot see. He means that community whose identity as the elect is apparent only to God's eyes.[9] We see the true church when we see the congregations of professing Christians. Faith has it that within the visible community the true church is there to be found. Where the Word is rightly preached and the sacraments rightly administered — and discipline rightly exercised[10] — there we must trust the church is to be found. The upshot of this — at least in Calvin's thinking — is that since we trust the elect to be there where two or three believers are pres-

---

9. Calvin, *Institutes of the Christian Religion,* ed. J. T. McNeill, trans. F. L. Battles, 2 vols. (Philadelphia: Westminster, 1960), 4.1.3-4, pp. 1014-16.

10. This third sign of the presence of the true church appears in subsequent Reformed confessions and catechisms.

ent, we are obliged to treat all as if they were the elect. Some later Calvinists sought in their accomplishments validating signs of their election. But according to Calvin, there is no justification for identifying anyone, *including self,* to be numbered among the reprobate. There are instances where Calvin fell short of his own teaching on this. However, technically the names and number of the elect are known only to God, and we are to live, and to encourage others to live, as persons chosen to serve. Election is not because of our performance of this or that act of piety. Election is because of sheer, sovereign, divinely strategic love.

The Church Spotless and Sinful

This is a tough belief to deal with respectfully and candidly. After all, we are dealing with the intimacy that defines all other subordinate intimacies. There is a reason why the church spoke of marriage as a "sacrament," the translation of *mysterion,* "mystery." Paul calls the union between Christ and the church a mystery (Eph. 4). He used this language for the ethical specificity that is to characterize the care a loving husband is to show toward his wife. It is to be self-sacrificing love. This passage was tragically misused when it was invoked to justify the degradation of women, to condone masculine arrogance. The verse was also misused to justify inhumane, impossible responsibilities placed on men. It is also sad to see the language of self-sacrificing love falling on bad times. It is now sometimes taken to mean unhealthy self-denial, a kind of pious obsequiousness. That is the opposite of the central point the passage is driving at.

That central point is that Christ loves the church so much that he was willing to give up his life for her, and that is the kind of love husbands are to practice toward their wives. Today we enjoy a more balanced view of genders than Paul was able to muster and still make some sense to his contemporaries. We know that the equation extends to saying also that wives are to love their husbands as Christ loves the church. Both spouses are equally forgiven and forgiving sinners whose life together manifests the maturity God intends. Their life together — accepting one another as Christ has accepted each — shows forth the quality of delight, freedom, peace, and justice God wills for all communities.

It is a tough question whether one can say of the church that she too is at once sinful and justified.[11] I respect the sensitivities of those who choose to say that individual members of the church sin but that Christ keeps spotless his bride, the church as a whole. Something more than semantics is at stake here. There are those — especially among Roman Catholics — who are right in emphasizing those verses that focus on Christ's keeping his body spotless until he returns in glory. I honor a certain stubborn healthiness that is offended by a crass, blasphemous denigration of the body of Christ. Of course, one has to take care not to impose an abstract definition of spotless as regards the church. For the church's spotlessness consists precisely in its being forgiven. Its spotlessness is not inherent, it is imputed to believers as Christ's totally, lavishly free gift.[12] Christ sanctifies the church unto himself. Therein, and therein alone, consists the church's spotlessness, and that is fully to be manifest at his coming again.

There is a sense in which the church's spotlessness is exactly in her being *simul justa et peccatrix.* How else can the church be immaculate? On what possible grounds could one otherwise de-

---

11. *Ecclesia simul justa et peccatrix,* corresponding to the view that a believer is at the same time sinner and righteous — *simul justa/justus et peccatrix/peccator.*

12. Cf. David Willis, *Notes on the Holiness of God* (Grand Rapids: Eerdmans, 2002), chapter entitled "The Hope of Holiness." Also the fine study by John Webster, *Holiness* (Grand Rapids: Eerdmans, 2003), and the twin volumes by Gordon Lathrop, *Holy People: A Liturgical Ecclesiology* (Minneapolis: Fortress, 1999) and *Holy Things: A Liturgical Theology* (Minneapolis: Fortress, 1993).

fine immaculateness? Here Hosea is to the point. His love for his wife is prophetic fidelity. There is no sentimentality in this costly devotion. There is no attempt to cover up the fact that like Hosea's wandering wife, Israel has gone off in her own promiscuous idolatry. In the history of interpretation, the church has applied Israel's behavior also to her, the church's, going far astray. In both cases, Israel's and the church's, the main point is not their flagrant infidelity. The main thing is the far greater reality of God's stubborn, unrelenting, steadfast love, of which Hosea's love toward his wife is a sign. This was seen in the church as a foreshadowing of Christ's relation to the church. Christ came into the world to save sinners, and by his acceptance we are brought back time and again — daily mortification and vivification — into that forgiveness and consequent new living in which alone the church's cleanness consists.

That is a freeing action on Christ's part. There is a boldness that comes with dwelling on the fidelity of God's love. Because of the love of the one with whom all things are possible, a believer is impelled forward to new feats of daring the seeming impossible. Remember Sarah and Mary when we think of that boldness to hear and do the apparently impossible. We are to welcome others as Christ has welcomed us — sinners cleansed, as robust hymns remind us, by his blood. "As far as the east is from the west, so far have I removed their sin," and so on.

We pay a dreadful price in our churches when we do not regularly recite and sing the whole of Psalm 51, and we pay a dreadful price if we mince the words of assurance after boldly confessing our sin. I think the subjunctive form is not strong enough, i.e., "May God grant. . . ." Real sinners need real declarations of pardon announced by real humans who are really used by the real God to proclaim with real authority Christ's accomplished forgiveness. Really! "In the name of Christ, I declare unto you that we are forgiven . . . ," and now let's get on with living as forgiven men and women![13] Away with the prissy, sniffy, thin-blooded, professionally meek who do not know either the depths of their sin or the heights of their recovery — and so quite miss the genuine meekness of which Christ spoke. The preacher in *Moby Dick* knew the difference between bilge despair and *"top gallant delight."*[14]

The Church Triumphant and Militant

As we noted above, Luther places great importance on the "Amen" believers say at the end of the Lord's Prayer. That small word both owns up to the truth of all that has preceded it and reminds believers that we are not alone. Our voices join the chorus of those who have prayed, do pray, and will in the future pray what Christ has taught. That, I take it, is what the distinction between the church militant and the church triumphant is all about. In this life, it is clear that believers struggle from day to day, moment to moment, to keep the faith — theirs and that of others. In those struggles, however, we are part of a far larger reality which is the full communion of saints. The Kirk, as the Scots Confession defines it, from the beginning has been, now is, and to the end of the world shall be. Here is the definition of the church from the Scots Confession: "As we believe in one God, Father, Son, and Holy Ghost, so we firmly believe that from the beginning there has been, now is, and to the end of the world shall be, one Kirk, that is to say, one company and multitude of men chosen by God, who rightly worship and embrace him by true faith in Jesus

13. Hence Will Campbell's summary of Christian ethics (as reported by Ann Chandler Willis and James and Julia Brawner) to a program committee at All Saints Church, Atlanta, during the civil rights conflicts: "You are a forgiven people! Now act like it!"

14. Herman Melville, *Moby Dick* (New York: Oxford University Press, 1947).

Christ, who is the only Head of the Kirk, even as it is the body and spouse of Jesus Christ."[15]

It used to be a common practice, useful to recover, to announce the death of this or that believer by saying so-and-so at such and such an hour "joined the church triumphant." A variation of that was to say that believers exchanged their burdens for a crown of glory. Belief in the reality of this larger communion emboldened believers with transforming patience in the midst of the trials here and now.[16]

The Four Promissory Marks of the Church

We can now say something about believing in the *"one, holy, catholic, apostolic" church.* Now we can see that in ticking off these characteristics we are not holding up a list of conditions that must be met in order for a sociologically observable movement to be the church. The "already–not fully" quality of life in the end times — the "for the time being" in the presence of the kingdom still drawing nigh — means that the blessed company of all the faithful people is not on hold until each characteristic is perfected. The faith of the faithful people is always in this life an expanding practice of living by informed trust. The church is that community which struggles by faith to live faithfully, and that means, as we have tried to indicate above, being covered by Christ's own faithfulness.

Unity, holiness, catholicity, apostolicity are not something the church "has." They *are the directions in which the church is growing.* The church is that repentant and forgiven and renewable and re-

15. Presbyterian Church U.S.A., *The Constitution, Part I, Book of Confessions* (Louisville: Office of the General Assembly, 1994), 3.16.

16. Cf. Harold A. Carter, *The Prayer Tradition of Black People* (Valley Forge, Pa.: Judson, 1976), and James H. Cone, *The Spirituals and the Blues* (New York: Seabury Press, 1972).

newing gathering of those who are assured of God's favor and goodness toward them — are heirs through hope of God's everlasting kingdom. To put it in professionally theological parlance, these four characteristics are eschatological realities: we live them more and more fully as we are drawn more and more to God's own fulfilling action in God's own time.

Each characteristic implies and entails the other characteristics. These four are not exhaustive, and they are not imperatives. They are indicatives which point to the ways the church is the glorious company of forgiven sinners through whom Christ is mediating his presence and activity. Each individual believes and comes to faith through the mediation — means — of grace. We come to know that Jesus is the Christ and to struggle to live out that reality in and through his body, the church. The unity of the church is a practice of being set apart for a witness, and it is sought and partially practiced by all believers in past time and times to come and everywhere. The criteria by which this unity is that of Christ and not of those who are wolves in sheep's clothes is tied to the message of the apostles.

The modern ecumenical movement was characterized by a recovery of an apostolic zeal for the unity and mission of the church. We think today, inevitably,[17] of the unity of the church in terms of which patterns are most to be sought and encouraged. Those models range from episcopal unity at the highest level (whatever that may be) to a so-called purely spiritual unity (whatever that may be). But the situation in the New Testament is perforce very fluid when it comes to specifying any single form of unity among Christians. No one was planning for centuries of

---

17. That is, given the great splits within the Western Church. I think of the scandal of two competing lines of popes, one of which had the good taste to locate in Provence. I think, even more, of the tragic split between Constantinople and Rome and the dreadful Western responsibility for its share of neglect resulting in the event of 1453, the fall of Constantinople to Islam.

such questions. They were concerned about the unity of Christians showing forth Christ's death until he comes, and that was expected to occur shortly. Living as a loving community was at the very heart of living in this world in the meantime. It was imperative to manifest the kind of life for which the gospel set men and women free. There were many congregations, and yet there was one church transcending localities. Believers gathered in many localities belonged to Christ and so to one another.

A new definition of localness and universality was being worked out. The church was one, made up of congregations scattered throughout the whole *oikoumene*. The congregations in one part of the inhabited earth heard of the plight of other congregations; an offering was taken up and given to those in *the* church elsewhere. Such generosity was a vivid instance of the complementarity of the gifts of the Spirit. These gifts were for the care and edification — including physical help — of the one community scattered through the then known world. This demonstration of the transcongregational unity of the church was grounded in early believers' understanding of the one Spirit present and active in different localities at the same time: one faith, one baptism, one Lord, and so on.

The imagery in the Bible for the church is remarkably rich: the people of God, the bride of Christ, those Christ called friends, the called-out ones, and so on. These various images emphasize part of the whole that takes into account other emphases. What term you use has a bearing on the debate over whether or not Christ founded the church. That is, the semantics of that question goes far in what answer one gives. The same is true of the debate over Jesus' interpretation of the movement he engendered and Paul's view and the so-called early Catholicism of the Pastoral Epistles.

There is plenty of warrant, in any case, for our embracing the language of the body of Christ, which Paul uses when confronting the threatening divisions among those who claim to be followers of Jesus Christ and Lord. For by that imagery Paul is pointing to the diversity-in-unity and unity-through-diversity which belong to the wholeness, health, and joy of Christians wherever they are gathered — in Corinth or Thessalonica or the churches of Asia Minor or Rome, and so on. Hence the exhortation that they should have the mind of Christ and cultivate their unity in him. I take this image to be the one which best informs what the creed is saying about believing in the one, holy, catholic, and apostolic church. That view of unity and diversity in Christ was the imagery perhaps more than any other that sustained the church through the persecutions and debates of its early years. Here is Paul's version of that imagery: the aim of the whole is love.

> Now there are varieties of gifts, but the same Spirit; and there are varieties of service, but the same Lord; and there are varieties of working, but it is the same God who inspires them all in every one. To each is given the manifestation of the Spirit for the common good. To one is given through the Spirit the utterance of wisdom, and to another the utterance of knowledge according to the same Spirit, to another faith by the same Spirit, to another gifts of healing by the one Spirit, to another the working of miracles, to another prophecy, to another the ability to distinguish between spirits, to another various kinds of tongues, to another the interpretation of tongues. All these are inspired by one and the same Spirit, who apportions to each one individually as he wills. For just as the body is one and has many members, and all the members of the body, though many, are one body, so it is with Christ. For by one Spirit we were all baptized into one body — Jews or Greeks, slaves or free — and all were made to drink of one Spirit. (1 Cor. 12:4-13)

The twin passage, one which sheds light on 1 Corinthians 12 and vice versa, is in Ephesians 4, whether the author be Paul himself or some sort of Pauline school or scribe. Again the overriding concern is that Christians live in the kind of harmony that proclaims the love of Christ to which also they, his followers, are called to manifest. Paul recommends the bond of peace, and does so from the bond of prison.

I therefore, a prisoner for the Lord, beg you to lead a life worthy of the calling to which you have been called, with all lowliness and meekness, with patience, forbearing one another in love, eager to maintain the unity of the Spirit in the bond of peace. There is one body and one Spirit, just as you were called to the one hope that belongs to your call, one Lord, one faith, one baptism, one God and Father of us all, who is above all and through all and in all. But grace was given to each of us according to the measure of Christ's gift. Therefore it is said, "When he ascended on high he led a host of captives, and he gave gifts to men." (In saying, "He ascended," what does it mean but that he had also descended into the lower parts of the earth? He who descended is he who also ascended far above all the heavens, that he might fill all things.) And his gifts were that some should be apostles, some prophets, some evangelists, some pastors and teachers, to equip the saints for the work of ministry, for building up the body of Christ, until we all attain to the unity of the faith and of the knowledge of the Son of God, to mature manhood, to the measure of the stature of the fulness of Christ; so that we may no longer be children, tossed to and fro and carried about with every wind of doctrine, by the cunning of men, by their craftiness in deceitful wiles. Rather, speaking the truth in love, we are to grow up in every way into him who is the head, into Christ, from whom the whole body, joined and knit together by every joint with which it is supplied, when each part is working properly, makes bodily growth and upbuilds itself in love. (Eph. 4:1-16)

Perhaps as much has been written about this passage as any other in Paul's writings, and much of that looks at it for clues to how the church is to be ordered: what the gifts are, what is the relation between gift and office, how many offices there are in the church, which are the higher and lower offices, whether there is any hierarchy of offices corresponding to the higher and lower gifts, and what "higher" and "lower" mean after all. But Paul's focus here is not primarily on details of church structure but on the fact that there is structure. Structure is a matter of the gifts being exercised for upbuilding believers into the body of Christ. Unity is part of the maturation in Christ.

The body imagery here places high importance on maturation and health, as proper working of each part for the whole, as the dynamics of the Spirit's gifting. We will return to this view of wholeness, salvation, when we take up the next section of the creed. Here I want simply to note that according to this imagery, there is structure and division of labor and particularity of contribution, highly valued for the health of the whole, to the common life of Christians. Life together in Christ is not amorphous: there is morphology to the church, growth according to an intended bodily structure and momentum. The Spirit builds us up, by the complementarity of gifts, into an ever greater maturity of service.

Whom the Whole Christ Includes

We have seen one sense in which the church is called "the body of Christ": that believers belong to Christ and belong to each other in so doing. However, we have also used the term "body of Christ" in another sense: that the church is one of the forms in which Christ's life is ongoing. The first sense refers to whose the church is. The second sense refers to that part of Christ's being which is his life in and through the members of which he is the head.

It is about this second sense of "the body of Christ" that I am now going to say something more. In a nutshell, it means: that *Christ mediates himself through* those united to himself by the bond of the Holy Spirit; and that this *union* of head and members is *one* reality, not two. That unified reality is spoken of as "the whole Christ" — *totus Christus*. There are good reasons for this doctrine that the church united to Christ is part of the whole Christ. There is a world of difference between (a) saying, correctly, that the Holy Spirit is the way the risen Christ unites us to himself and (b) saying, wrongly, that the Holy Spirit is what we receive instead of Christ. There is also a world of difference between (a) saying, correctly, that the church is a means by which are extended the saving effects of the whole course of Christ's obedience and (b) saying, imprecisely, that the church is the extension of the incarnation. The church is neither an extension of the incarnation nor a movement of some spirit that ultimately has as its central reality something other than the love of God known above all in Christ and his benefits. The church is one of the ways — the defining way, but not the only way — Christ is present, is benevolently active far beyond our fondest imagination. That is what it means to confess that Christ dwells in us and we in him. That is what it means to confess with Paul that "I live, yet not I, but Christ in me." We must also go on to say "the church lives, yet not the church, but Christ in the church" — and beyond it. Remember again the assurance that is part of the prayer ordinarily spoken after Communion — that we are very members of his mystical body and that he dwells in us and we in him evermore.

CHAPTER EIGHT

The Future of Forgiveness

We acknowledge one baptism for the forgiveness of sins. We look for the resurrection of the dead and the life of the world to come.

These lines form a unity. They refer to three benefits of the knowledge of God the Holy Spirit. They confess the connection between baptism and forgiveness, between forgiveness and resurrection, and between resurrection and what Christians ultimately hope for. This is the flow of the Christian life. It is not a series of steps in being saved but an unfolding, a maturing, of that which is already ratified in baptism and is therefore to be nurtured with joyful, imaginative perseverance.

To What We Are Drawn Forward

Before we consider what baptism is good for, we need to lift up an image that healthily shapes our thinking about active compassion (for that is what forgiveness is) and the discipline of looking for the life of the world to come (for that is the expansive scope of Christian hope).

Ambitious speculations about individuals' survivability and the trappings of heaven have come to determine more of our thinking about the future life than we realize. In the Bible, however, the life of the world to come has mainly to do with the coming of God's manifest, unmistakable, long-sought, struggled-for shalom for the whole of creation. Nowhere, I think, is this promise more evocatively put than in the description of what will happen to creatures with the coming of the Messiah, in Isaiah's vision of the Holy Mountain, the Peaceable Kingdom.

There shall come forth a shoot from the stump of Jesse, and a branch shall grow out of his roots. And the Spirit of the LORD shall rest upon him, the spirit of wisdom and understanding, the spirit of counsel and might, the spirit of knowledge and the fear of the LORD. And his delight shall be in the fear of the LORD. He shall not judge by what his eyes see, or decide by what his ears hear; but with righteousness he shall judge the poor, and decide with equity for the meek of the earth; and he shall smite the earth with the rod of his mouth, and with the breath of his lips he shall slay the wicked. Righteousness shall be the girdle of his waist, and faithfulness the girdle of his loins. The wolf shall dwell with the lamb, and the leopard shall lie down with the kid, and the calf and the lion and the fatling together, and a little child shall lead them. The cow and the bear shall feed; their young shall lie down together; and the lion shall eat straw like the ox. The sucking child shall play over the hole of the asp, and the weaned child shall put his hand on the adder's den. They shall not hurt or destroy in all my holy mountain; for the earth shall be full of the knowledge of the LORD as the waters cover the sea. (Isa. 11:1-9)[1]

1. The presentation and translation of this remarkable poetry are not at all

There are many layers of meaning to this text. I mention only six. First, the whole condition envisioned is the result of the coming of the Messiah, the one anointed by the Spirit. Second, the Messiah is identified as the new shoot coming from an old trunk. The hiddenness-apparentness dynamic of God's saving activity is underlined once again. Third, the condition resulting from the Messiah's presence is noticeable, startling, inescapable by its chief characteristic, namely, the replacement of enmity with peace among all creatures, the most unlikely pairs co-dwelling safely: "They shall not hurt or destroy in all my holy mountain." That also means the carnivores become plant-eaters! Fourth, the whole transformation is proclaimed and recognized because it is a fulfillment of God's promise of steadfast love: it comes about as a result of God's unrelenting strategic designs. Fifth, there are uses made in both Testaments of mountains, including where the covenants are made at Sinai and Shechem before Ebal and Gerizim, for the transfiguration, and so on. This does not mean that other imagery, especially that of a city, is not used canonically. It is, however, a deliberate choice that I make[2] here to lift up, as it were, the image of the Holy Mountain. One of the image's strengths is precisely its being so mixed a metaphor. The Holy Mountain is a

---

self-evident. For one thing, I have altered the way the Revised Standard Version has it. The latter has shown the passage's poetic cadences — as we use them today — to make sure the reader gets the words as poetry. As orally recited, of course, the vocal inflections indicated this. For another thing, the difference between capital *S* and minuscule *s* for "spirit" is a bit too helpful. The translators have been too helpful in assigning a capital letter to the Spirit of the Lord which comes upon the Messiah and the spirit of wisdom and counsel and so on. An uncapitalized or minusculized text obviously does not so readily make that distinction. I have also chosen not to include the verse numbers. I want the poetry to flow as much as possible so that we get the passage as a liturgical whole.

2. Maybe because I cannot get out of my mind Gregory of Nazianzus's *Theological Orations,* included in E. R. Hardy, ed., *Christology of the Later Fathers* (Philadelphia: Westminster, 1954), pp. 128-214.

Peaceable Kingdom. The reason there shall be no hurting or destroying in all the Lord's Holy Mountain is because "the earth shall be full of the knowledge of the LORD as the waters cover the sea." Sixth, the future continuity and discontinuity of individuals are derivative parts of the more inclusive peace of all on the Holy Mountain. There is relatively little that we can say about the shape of an individual's life after death. However, when we claim the old covenant is fulfilled in the new, we locate our personal hope in the context of an inclusive shalom. Our lives are hidden in Christ: that is all we finally know and finally need to know. The Holy Mountain image colors my interpretation of other aspects, and other descriptions, of the life of the world — the *world* — to come. Our lives are hidden in Christ because we are located and placed in him; we *belong* in him. That condition is both proclaimed and confirmed in the act of baptism.

Baptism and Forgiveness

Baptism itself is not a single completed action, though there is obviously a punctiliar quality to it: I was baptized, you were baptized, they were baptized, and that is an irreversible fact, a done deal. The very nature of what is done has a forward dynamic to it. The significance of that singularly done deal grows on one as one actively remembers one's baptism, actively remembers that one does not belong to sin, death, and the devil, but to one another. Ultimately we belong body and soul to our faithful Savior Jesus Christ — as the Heidelberg Catechism reminds us.[3]

This punctiliar-plus-growth quality of baptism is not unlike

---

3. Cf. Question and Answer 1 of the Heidelberg Catechism. F. H. Klooster, *A Mighty Comfort: The Christian Faith according to the Heidelberg Catechism* (Grand Rapids: CRC Publications, 1990).

the artist's act of getting a painting, sculpture, rug, lace, concerto, or piece of pottery done plus the growing interaction with that art so that the moment of artistic creativity is set in motion and has a momentum of its own which goes far beyond the initial act. This is of comfort, consolation, and encouragement, strengthening my assurance of our own condition before God. But it is of immense comfort when it comes to the assurance of our loved ones' conditions. They belong to Christ. Their status is defined benevolently, no matter what. Nothing can now separate them from the love of God in Christ Jesus.

Of course, they and we do not begin to be the objects of God's steadfast love when we are baptized. We are baptized, brought to that moment and that new visibility in the life of the believing community, because God's steadfast love has worked its sovereign way already in our lives. Our loved ones are "signed," "sealed," and "delivered." Baptism is an act of sealing the realization of their and my deliverance. It is the same as conversion in the sense that, yes, one can point to this or that acknowledgment of God's love and its consequences. Growth in grace, however, means being converted over and over again, what used to be called daily mortification and vivification.

When we say there is one baptism for the remission of sin, we are recognizing the connection between baptism, repentance, and forgiveness. There are persuasive arguments to be made for both practices of the one baptism, infant baptism and believer's baptism.[4] Often the reason given in favor of believer's baptism is that by a certain age young people — not infants — know enough about the *content of the faith* to embrace it in a witting act. That reason is solid enough; but the more serious question is whether the person being baptized is mature enough to know *what it means*

---

4. See David Willis, ed., *Baptism: Decision and Growth* (Philadelphia: Office of the General Assembly, 1972).

to repent. In the earliest accounts of baptism, the question was not so much about the identity of those being baptized. They knew they belonged to the community that belonged to the Messiah. Rather, the most urgent question was, did they realize the seriousness of their condition if they were not forgiven — especially the frightful implications of not recognizing the presence of the kingdom of God ushered in by Jesus the Messiah? In response to Peter's proclamation on Pentecost, the cry of those convicted of their sin was, "What must we do to be saved?" The answer was, "Repent and be baptized."

Repentance means not just feeling sorry for misdemeanors. It means turning completely around and heading in the opposite direction, and that means entering into the way of costly discipleship. So, if parents and other believing members of a congregation choose to be party to baptizing children, they bring to that action not just the convictions of informed, witting belief. They also bring a vicarious repentance in which they pledge to help the person — adult as well as infant — grow. The baptized and baptizing community is a knowing and repentant community. They know to whom they most belong, and therefore they know the seriousness of the condition from which Jesus is the deliverer.

The Penultimate Fact of Sin

Forgiveness entails more than adjustment to one's dysfunctional proclivities! Forgiveness entails costly deliverance. The question remains, however, deliverance from what or whom? Well, for openers, deliverance from the hand of Pharaoh. I say "for openers" advisedly, because it is the same benevolently intrusive God who overrides every form of bondage to let his people go. That exodus from Egypt is prototypical for Israel. It is at the very heart of Israel's remembered salvation narrative. It is prototypical for understanding the nature of the new form of the old covenant and for understanding the magnitude of new freedoms. Radical deliverances, personal and societal, are defined by the exodus experience. Everything from which Christ graciously delivers us is what we mean by sin, and sin is most defined and recognized in the deliverance from it. The Nicene Creed names it. Forgiveness is not for finitude and fragility and corruption. Forgiveness is for sin.

Note that this is the first time in the creed that sin has been explicitly named. Yes, of course, it is in the background all along. It was implied when we confessed that Jesus Christ "for us and our salvation" came down — even if we recognize that salvation has mainly, but not exclusively, to do with righting the consequences of sin. It is only after we have experienced the good news as applying also to us that we can face the fact of sin with the serious attention it deserves. Sin is that from which we are continually experiencing deliverance. Transgression, death, and the devil are defined as those over which Christ has triumphed. In baptism we affirm that triumph and pledge to live by its truth.

The whole of Christian discipleship is the active remembrance of our baptism. I have, above, made it amply clear, I think, that this triumph over sin, death, and the devil is an accomplished fact that still has to be lived out, practiced, matured in imperfectly all our life long.[5] It is a reality that we already rejoice over; and yet it is a reality whose fullness lies ahead of us and is time after time desperately illusive. The more we realize the assurance of our salvation, the more we realize the depth and ingenuity of that from

---

5. Cf. Heidelberg Catechism: "Q. 56. What do you believe concerning 'the forgiveness of sins'? A. That, for the sake of Christ's reconciling work, God will no more remember my sins or the sinfulness with which I have to struggle all my life long; but that he graciously imparts to me the righteousness of Christ so that I may never come into condemnation." Presbyterian Church U.S.A., *The Constitution, Part I, Book of Confessions* (Louisville: Office of the General Assembly, 1994), p. 37.

which we have been delivered. The gospel is the presupposition of the seriousness of the law, and in this way the law — to use Paul's framework — is part of the good news.

Sin and the Drive to Control Others

One of the chief forms of sin we need deliverance from is the need to control others as we would not be controlled by them. This is a tricky business to deal with fairly. Much depends on what we mean by the terms of the discussion. The connection, however, between sin and the drive to control others is too destructive not to be addressed.

We need to distinguish between two senses of the drive to control. One kind of control belongs to maturation. It means taking charge of one's life in the sense of owning up to the consequences of one's own choices and learning from them. It means not being symbiotically dependent on others, not cultivating neediness in order to remain at an arrested stage of development. Now, none of us is ever finished with this vocation to sane independence. There are long seasons for all of us when we cannot, for various reasons, take charge of our own lives. In fact, part of maturing is learning to differentiate those things we can handle ourselves and those things for which we need to admit our need. There is irony here. Sometimes maturation in the right kind of control means learning to admit our need for help from others.

Then there is the second kind of drive to control, the one that belongs to dysfunction, to stunted growth, to diseased psyches and psychosomatic malaise. This drive to control is especially serpentine because it often is *masked as love* and is often *practiced unconsciously* as well as deliberately.

This drive to control others is love gone haywire. If a person is so terribly loving, caring, active in what he or she thinks to be your good, it is extremely difficult to say "Thanks but no thanks." Manipulative omnipresence and omni-doing-for-others is one of the things from which the gospel frees men and women, and that freeing power of the gospel takes place from top to bottom of our personhood.

The drive to control others as we would not have them control us is a deeply rooted tendency that can be redirected into healthful expressions only when we face it in ourselves. The soil, as it were, in which this destructive form of control takes root is a person's insecurity about his or her worth. Oh, of course, there are many components to fundamental doubt about one's worth, standing, esteem. We will be saying more about injustice which breeds more injustice, about poverty which breeds more poverty, about abuse which breeds more abuse, about violence which breeds more violence. We here are deliberately speaking about the psychological dynamics of insecurity turned fatal, but we are doing so not as a substitute for acknowledging the social ethics, the prophetic indicatives, revealed in the Decalogue.

Here, however, is the place to note that one of the major components of this destructive insecurity is the disparity between (a) an idealized image of self and (b) what we see in the mirror. The gospel and law help drive us to the exposure of our true condition, and that truthfulness is itself the beginning of health — and the beginning of the conflict with self which comes with getting healthy. That idealized image of self is partly the set of expectations others have of us, and partly the set of expectations we use to measure our own worth. When that self-image is radically upended (as it will be, and must be for growth to the next stage of maturation), the result is painful insecurity.[6]

The easiest, and falsest, answer to this insecurity is to scramble

6. Cf. Monica Furlong, *Christian Uncertainties* (Cambridge, Mass.: Cowley, 1982).

for control whereby we try to allay fears about our worth by controlling others around us. This nexus is cut through by the assurance that in Christ, all that God wishes for our good has been lavishly granted. What each and every person most hungers for and is most loath to lose has been lavishly given sevenfold times seven. It is one thing to recognize this dynamic. It is another thing to practice it day in and day out. In this practice, recognizing the third part of Christian freedom is of great help. To wean self away from the need to control others is to lighten up about things that are of secondary and tertiary importance. That is a letting go, an unburdening. This unburdening is not unlike what the Indians do with the armor carried by the Jesuit in that superb movie *The Mission.*

I take the hunger for controllable security to be quite different from the control that comes from trusting God to be ultimately in charge. Knowing that God's benevolence is the essential fact of our lives frees us to take responsibility for our own lives, to make hard decisions and stick with the consequences of them. We are freed to practice the ways of the maturity that is a mark of the greatest virtue, love. This is part of the paradox of the Christian life as a journey. To lose oneself is to find oneself. To give up egocentric control is to practice the diaconal control of the common life. In that mutual service we refine ways of caring for others, including respecting their independence. By the same token, in this mutual service we also learn a terribly difficult thing for many: we learn to accept the care others have for us, including their respecting our healthy independence.

Original Righteousness and the Decalogue

Righteousness is original and sin is unoriginal. The misleading term "original sin" originally (!) meant that all humans are caught up in the nexus of universal sin, universal in the sense that no one is exempt from its ravages. Augustine, and others, made the unfortunate move of accounting for this ubiquity of sin in terms of biological solidarity through procreation. That was unimaginative enough, but the misunderstanding was enormously compounded when the solidarity of sin was mainly ascribed to what goes on in sexual intercourse. I use "what goes on" because it was not always clear and consistent what was wrong with what otherwise would seem to be a good gift from the good God. Was the sinful part somehow the act itself, was it the shame that Genesis says Adam and Eve had, was it the loss of paradise innocence, was it the pleasure which tempted us to take more delight in each other than in God, or was it something else or all of the above?

It was right for Augustine and others to point out how sexual intercourse exposed men and women to their vulnerability as few other acts do. The abuse of love, the manipulation of another human being, is an ever present danger. But it was less than felicitous to single out sexual relations as thereby more prone to sin than other activities — say economic, racial, paternalistic, maternalistic, materialistic, militaristic misuses of power. To this day the *misunderstood* doctrine of "original sin" reinforces a preoccupation with sinful abuse of our good sexuality. This tragic misunderstanding is still perpetuated by official teachings in some denominations. Right enjoyment of sexuality and freely exercised joy in another person are difficult enough for everyone, believer or not. The church's frequent confusion on the matter cannot be said to have been of much help.

Ironically, fixation on sexual sins minimizes their real seriousness. Adultery can be as much a sin of omission as commission, as when a person manipulatively withholds sexual relations from his or her mate. In both forms, adultery is lusting after another — perhaps lusting after one's manipulative power in withholding affection. Adultery, in its many forms and like the other behaviors proscribed in the Ten Commandments, is a way of denying accountability before God for the care we are to have for others. If we say we are not accountable, we are walking in the dark and the truth is not in us. Adultery is a sin, no matter how one may try to rationalize or excuse it. It is covetousness in action, of which David's hunger for Bathsheba is a classic instance. It is a form of gluttony, taking something that does not belong to one and consuming it as if it did. That means that those who think themselves free from this sin deceive themselves dangerously.

God gives the Decalogue to order our common life as people of this God and not another. The Ten Commandments (or the Ten Words) are permissions of structured freedom.[7] They are all elucidations of the first word (or preamble, depending on how people number the ten): "I am the Lord your God. You shall have no other gods before me." Each commandment warns against a breach of the boundaries essential to the common life of those who belong not to themselves or other humans but to the God whose call makes them into a people. The free sanity of the common life is violated by killing; stealing on small and large scales; lying, which includes withholding part of the truth; messing with God's name and calling the gods God; despising one's parents and not helping them in their independent dignity; and imagining and clinging to portable idols. The list is not exhaustive, but it is enough to give the people the picture. If ten are too hard to remember or too prone to nitpicking denial, the summary covers the ground: You shall love the Lord your God with all your heart and soul and mind, and your neighbor as yourself.

All these come replete with delectable variations, and whoever thinks himself or herself innocent of even one of the sins

7. See Barth's treatment of the commandments as gracious permissions, in *Church Dogmatics* I/1–IV/4 (Edinburgh: T. & T. Clark, 1936-69), II/2, par. 36-39. Note the different settings of the Decalogue in the Exodus and the Deuteronomy texts. Note also the difference between the Lutheran and Reformed ways of numbering the two tables of the Law.

named in the Decalogue seriously deludes himself or herself. Self-righteousness is a doubly serious sin because it places self in the position that God alone is to occupy in our common life. God alone has the right to judge, much less to wreak vengeance. Taking revenge to oneself is a colossal effrontery to God's gracious sovereignty. Were we to await our worthiness to be forgiven, we should be living proofs of the killing power of the law. None stands before God except through the offices of the one Mediator. Yet, seeing that we do indeed have that Mediator, "touched at all points as we are yet without sin," we may come to the throne of grace with unfeigned repentance. Another paradox of the Christian life is that, freed from the condemning necessity of fulfilling the law — not a jot or tittle of which shall pass away — we find ourselves practicing the freedom of growing in fulfilling the commandments. That is where the Reformed branch of the catholic church is right on target: the third use of the law is to guide believers in their growth in grace.[8]

Costly Repentance

Another word about forgiveness: it is costly, and the greater the sin the greater the cost. I do not mean costly in the sense that a bully may say, "You'll pay for this." I mean that the commandments are given for a reason — the well-being of life together as God's people. The breaking of the commandment brings with it, as it were, its own consequences. Others and self are wounded, sickened, de-

---

8. Cf. Calvin's treatment of the three uses of the Law: the civil use to order society, the pedagogical use to drive us to Christ, and the third use, which is to guide Christians in their growth in sanctification. *Institutes of the Christian Religion* 2.7.6-15. Compare these to Calvin's description of the three parts of Christian freedom: freedom from works righteousness, freedom to practice the Law, and freedom to be indifferent about indifferent things. *Institutes* 3.19.

based, saddened, angered in a downward spiral of violence to others and to self. Repentance is not just an apology, nor is it done only once. Repentance is a daily business. It is not perpetual recrimination of self. On the contrary, it is a matter of continual alertness about those things we have to fight all our life long. It is the practice (to take a page from Alcoholics Anonymous) of being recovering bond servants of this or that form of sin to which we were most prone — and of doing the best we can to take care for those we have hurt in the process of our effrontery.

This is where the costliness of sin and the costliness of forgiveness come together. We are surely not saved by our repentance; but convicted of our sin by the gospel, we naturally[9] seek ways of caring for those — including self — who are wounded by sin. That costliness is the exact opposite of harboring our regrets and cultivating them and reopening wounds so they never heal. It costs to put past sins behind us. It costs to be accountable for moving forward with the details of living as forgiven sinners. Part of the costliness of costly grace is the discipline daily to cherish God's forgiveness more than to dwell on one's manifest sins.

It is a common and very powerful form of pride to think that our sins are stronger than God's grace, and to live more in awe before our sins and the condemnation of others than before God's restoring love and acceptance by other members of the body of Christ. The old-timers made a wise distinction between two kinds of consequences of sin: guilt and harm.[10] These ancients knew that we can have the *guilt* wiped away by forgiveness, but that we still have to live with sin's *harm,* sin's destructive consequences to other and self. Forgiveness is not just getting free *from* guilt. It is

---

9. See Bonhoeffer's treatment of the recovery of the natural, in *Ethics,* ed. Eberhard Bethge (New York: Macmillan, 1961).

10. See the treatment of the relation between *culpa,* "guilt," and *poena,* "harm," in Malcolm France, *The Paradox of Guilt: A Christian Study of the Relief of Self-Hatred* (Philadelphia: United Church Press, 1967).

that. But it is primarily being free of guilt *for*. Forgiveness is *in order to live healingly*. Guilt that is not let go hampers what the forgiven sinner is freed for: new life.

Christ's Resurrection and Ours

With that ever in mind, we can now turn to the profound arrangement of the creed by which the content of forgiveness of sin is likened to the resurrection of the dead. This is a matter of being clear about the implications of being joined to Christ in resurrection since we are joined to him in his death. That is what it means to be raised from the dead: to share, at a creaturely level and magnitude, at an accommodated understanding and therefore disciplined humility, Christ's own resurrection — the first fruit which brings with it other ripening to new life.

I have just spoken of the resurrection *from* the dead, but the creed says we look for the resurrection *of* the dead. That intensifies the scandal, for it means that those who are dead will be raised from the dead, will be made alive again. We are not talking here only about Christ's resurrection: that we already confessed in the second article. We are talking about the destiny of the many after death, after the stopped living of people, after the heart and brain and all the rest stop working and quickly decompose. I have no idea what "the resurrection of the dead" means, except that it is analogous to the seed that drops into the ground and shows up next as a plant — that is as far as Paul goes in his imagery. We know what that is like, and we know what it means to risk next year's crop by throwing seed into the ground and taking the risk of losing everything. There is no new life that does not go through such a burial: vivification comes through mortification.

On the one hand, we ought not begrudge those who find comfort in the literal iconography of graves opening and formerly dead people getting up and moving around. On the other hand, we can be guided by Tillich's wisdom about respecting symbols that have their own timeliness and so are not to be discarded just because they do not ring a bell with us at this or that time. Symbols, however, are pointers to the far greater reality in which they partake. The resurrection of the dead is a symbol for the far greater reality that is the life of the world to come. Only part of the life of the world to come is the dead in some sense coming alive again.

Life after death is an existential reality for believers. Very often it is only when this or that situation seems hopelessly beyond repair, only when we have done all we can to pump life into something and failed, only when we are compelled to let go of something or someone — then and only then there comes about a totally unexpected, previously unimaginable renewal of life. I do not mean to reduce the experience of death and resurrection to psychological or sociological dimensions. However, I do mean that since we already share in the new life in Christ, we are not left with an arbitrary meaning of the phrase "resurrection of the dead."[11]

The important verb in this last sentence of the creed is "to look for, to expect." We have already seen how permeated the New Testament is with the believing community's *living forward* to Christ's return in glory to judge the living and the dead. Yet look: we are living forward *to the world to come*. We face forward — we live *futureward* — with confidence because we already know who the coming one is. We already know his favor and goodness toward us. That is why it is important in the liturgy to proclaim

---

11. The sung "Credo" — say, in Bach's Mass in B minor — also gives me an analogical experience whereby I am made to participate imperfectly, but surely, in the reality to which the words, notes, and musicians point. See Jaroslav Pelikan, *Bach among the Theologians* (Philadelphia: Fortress, 1986).

the following mystery of the faith: "Christ has died, Christ has risen, and Christ will come again." God is not pulling a switch on us. We are in for the purifying presence of Christ in a new, more direct, less hidden way. This is a matter of greater rejoicing, and of sober fear.

Anyone who discounts the judgment yet to come sorely mistakes the depth of the predicament Christ's return will expose and correct. There will be an accounting and manifest right-making. The upheavals and changing places promised in the Magnificat will be completely fulfilled. Christian freedom comes with accountability. That means that the more we are the recipients of God's freeing message, the more we are answerable for our blessings. That we do not know the shape of this accountability does not mean we can escape it. What we do know for sure is that the same one to whom we are accountable is the one of whose sovereign benevolence — costly benevolence — we are assured. The judgment to come is, after all, located by the creed in the section on what it means to believe in Jesus Christ.

When it comes to the details of the life of the world to come, a kind of agnosticism is healthy. The creed deals with this part of the truth sparingly, austerely, as if to prevent us from confusing nonessential details with the essential reality of our hope. The creed does not end on a speculative, unsure note. The brevity of what it has to say about the life of the world to come is not unlike the power of minimalism in art. Less is more: the truth is best told by uncluttering the mind of fanciful construction. It is enough to know that the world to come belongs to the Lord of the world already here and now, the very same Jesus Christ Lord. Knowing that, we know one thing for sure: ineffable joy shall abound. "The Spirit and the Bride say, 'Come.' And let him who hears say, 'Come.' And let him who is thirsty come, let him who desires take the water of life without price" (Rev. 22:17).

Mostly English Bibliography

✠　✠

Allen, Diogenes. *Philosophy for Understanding Theology.* Atlanta: John Knox, 1985.

Alston, Wallace M. *The Church.* Atlanta: John Knox, 1984.

————, ed. *Theology in the Service of the Church: Essays in Honor of Thomas W. Gillespie.* Grand Rapids: Eerdmans, 2000.

Anderson, Bernhard. *Understanding the Old Testament.* Englewood Cliffs, N.J.: Prentice-Hall, 1957.

Anselm of Canterbury. *Fides Quaerens Intellectum: id est, Proslogion* . . . Paris: J. Vrin, 1992.

————. "Why God Became Man." In *A Scholastic Miscellany,* edited by Eugene R. Fairweather, pp. 100-183. Philadelphia: Westminster, 1956.

Aulen, Gustav. *Christus Victor.* New York: Macmillan, 1951.

Balthasar, Hans Urs von. *Presence and Thought: Essay on the Religious Philosophy of Gregory of Nyssa.* San Francisco: Ignatius, 1995.

————. *Truth Is Symphonic: Aspects of Christian Pluralism.* San Francisco: Ignatius, 1987.

Barth, Karl. *Church Dogmatics.* Vols. I/1–IV/4. Edinburgh: T. & T. Clark, 1936-69.

————. *Fides Quaerens Intellectum: Anselm's Proof* . . . Richmond, Va.: John Knox, 1960.

————. *The Göttingen Dogmatics: Instruction in the Christian Religion.* Vol. 1. Grand Rapids: Eerdmans, 1991.

————. *The Humanity of God.* Richmond, Va.: John Knox, 1960.

————. *Die Kirchliche Dogmatik.* Vols. I/1–IV/1. Zollikon-Zürich: Evangelischer Verlag, 1932ff.

————. *The Word of God and the Word of Man.* New York: Harper and Bros., 1957.

Battles, Ford Lewis. "God Was Accommodating Himself to Human Capacity." In

Readings in Calvin's Theology, edited by Donald K. McKim, pp. 24-42. Grand Rapids: Baker, 1984.

Baynes, Pauline. *The Nicene Creed Illustrated by Pauline Baynes.* Grand Rapids: Eerdmans, 2003.

Bernanos, Georges. *Diary of a Country Priest.* New York: Macmillan, 1937.

Bernhardt, Reinhold, and David Willis. "Theologia Crucis." In *Evangelisches Kirchenlexikon,* edited by E. Fahlbusch et al., vol. 7, cols. 734-36. Göttingen: Vandenhoeck & Ruprecht, 1996.

Bethge, Eberhard. *Dietrich Bonhoeffer.* New York: Harper and Row, 1970.

Bieler, Andre. *The Politics of Hope.* Grand Rapids: Eerdmans, 1974.

Bonhoeffer, Dietrich. *The Communion of Saints.* New York: Harper and Row, 1963.

————. *The Cost of Discipleship.* New York: Macmillan, 1965.

————. *Ethics.* Edited by Eberhard Bethge. New York: Macmillan, 1961.

————. *Letters and Papers from Prison.* Enlarged edition by Eberhard Bethge. New York: Macmillan, 1972.

————. *Life Together.* New York: Harper, 1954.

Botman, H. Russel. "Theology after Apartheid: Paradigms and Progress in South African Public Theologies." In *Theology in the Service of the Church: Essays in Honor of Thomas W. Gillespie,* edited by Wallace M. Alston, pp. 36-51. Grand Rapids: Eerdmans, 2000.

Braaten, Carl, and Robert W. Jenson, eds. *Christian Dogmatics.* 2 vols. Philadelphia: Fortress, 1984.

Bright, John. *A History of Israel.* 3rd ed. Philadelphia: Westminster, 1981.

Brown, Peter. *Augustine of Hippo.* Berkeley: University of California Press, 1969.

Brueggemann, Walter, and Patrick D. Miller. *The Covenanted Self: Explorations in Law and Covenant.* Minneapolis: Fortress, 1999.

Brunnner, Emil. *The Mediator.* Philadelphia: Westminster, 1947.

Buber, Martin. *I and Thou.* 2nd. ed. New York: Charles Scribner's Sons, 1958.

Buechner, Frederick. *Listening to Your Life.* San Francisco: Harper, 1992.

Burnaby, John. *The Belief of Christendom* [on the Nicene Creed]. London: SPCK, 1975.

Calvin, John. *Institutes of the Christian Religion.* Edited by J. T. McNeill. Translated by F. L. Battles. 2 vols. Philadelphia: Westminster, 1960.

————. *Institution de la Religion Chrétienne.* Edited by J.-D. Benoit. 5 vols. Paris: J. Vrin, 1957-.

————. *Johannis Calvini Opera Selecta.* Edited by P. Barth and W. Niesel. 5 vols. Munich: Chr. Kaiser, 1926-36.

Carr, Anne E. *Transforming Grace: Christian Tradition and Women's Experience.* San Francisco: Harper, 1988.

Carter, Harold A. *The Prayer Tradition of Black People.* Valley Forge, Pa.: Judson, 1976.

Charry, Ellen. *By the Renewing of Your Minds: The Pastoral Function of Christian Doctrine.* New York: Oxford University Press, 1997.

Ciardi, John, and Miller Williams. *How Does a Poem Mean?* 2nd ed. Boston: Houghton Mifflin, 1975.

Cogeval, Guy. *Vuillard: Post-Impressionist Master.* New York: Abrams, 2002.

Cone, James H. *The Spirituals and the Blues.* New York: Seabury Press, 1972.

Cone, James H., and Gayraud S. Wilmore, eds. *Black Theology: A Documentary History.* Maryknoll, N.Y.: Orbis, 1993.

Congar, Yves. *I Believe in the Holy Spirit.* New York: Seabury Press, 1983.

Danielou, Jean. *Gospel Message and Hellenistic Culture . . . before the Council of Nicaea.* Vol. 2. Philadelphia: Westminster, 1973.

De Gruchy, John W. *Liberating Reformed Theology.* Grand Rapids: Eerdmans, 1991.

De Journal, Rouet, ed. *Enchiridion Patristicum.* Barcelona: Herder, 1959.

Dempsey Douglass, Jane. *Women, Freedom, and Calvin.* Philadelphia: Westminster, 1985.

Dempsey Douglass, Jane, and James F. Kay, eds. *Women, Gender, and Christian Community.* Louisville: Westminster John Knox, 1997.

De Senarclens, Jacques. *Heirs of the Reformation.* Philadelphia: Westminster, 1963.

DeVries, Dawn. "The Incarnation and the Sacramental Word." In *Toward the Future of Reformed Theology,* edited by D. Willis and M. Welker, pp. 386-405. Grand Rapids: Eerdmans, 1999.

De Waal, Esther. *The Celtic Vision.* Petersham, Mass.: St. Bede's Publications, 1990.

―――. "The Cistercians." In *A Definitive History of Abbey Dore,* edited by Ron Shoesmith and Ruth Richardson, pp. 7-14. Little Logaston Woonton Almeley, Herefordshire: Logaston Press, 1997.

―――. *Living with Contradiction.* San Francisco: Harper and Row, 1989.

―――. *Lost in Wonder.* Norwich: Canterbury Press, 2003.

―――. *Seeking God: The Way of St. Benedict.* Collegeville, Minn.: Liturgical Press, 1984.

Dillenberger, Jane. *Image and Spirit in Sacred and Secular Art.* New York: Crossroad, 1990.

Dillenberger, John. *God Hidden and Revealed.* Philadelphia: Muhlenberg, 1953.

Dillistone, Frederick W. *Christian Understanding of the Atonement.* Philadelphia: Westminster, 1968.

―――. *The Holy Spirit in the Life of Today.* Philadelphia: Westminster, 1947.

―――. *Jesus Christ and His Cross.* Philadelphia: Westminster, 1953.

————. *The Power of Symbols in Religion and Culture*. New York: Crossroad, 1986.

————. *Religious Experience and Christian Faith*. London: SCM, 1981.

————. *The Structure of the Divine Society*. London: Lutterworth, 1951.

Dowey, Edward A., Jr. *A Commentary on the Confession of 1967 and an Introduction to "The Book of Confessions."* Philadelphia: Westminster, 1968.

Duff, Nancy. *Humanization and the Politics of God: The Koinonia Ethics of Paul Lehmann*. Grand Rapids: Eerdmans, 1992.

Dulles, Avery. *Models of the Church*. Expanded edition. New York: Doubleday, Image Books, 1987.

Ebeling, Gerhard. *The Study of Theology*. Philadelphia: Fortress, 1978.

Edwards, Jonathan. *The Works of Jonathan Edwards*. 2 vols. New Haven: Yale University Press, 1957-.

New York: Norton, 1973.

Eliot, T. S. *On Poetry and Poets*. New York: Farrar, Straus and Giroux, Noonday, 1961.

Ellman, Richard, and Robert O'Clair, eds., *The Norton Anthology of Modern Poetry*. Episcopal Church. *The Book of Common Prayer*. New York: Church Hymnal Corporation and Seabury Press, 1977.

Evans, Francis. "The Engineer Monks." In *A Definitive History of Abbey Dore*, edited by Ron Shoesmith and Ruth Richardson, pp. 139-48. Little Logaston Woonton Almeley, Herefordshire: Logaston Press, 1997.

Fairchild, Roy W. *Finding Hope Again*. San Francisco: Harper and Row, 1980.

Florovsky, Georges. *Ways of Russian Theology*. Part 1. New York: Nordland, 1979.

Forde, Gerhard O. "Luther's Theology of the Cross." In *Christian Dogmatics*, edited by C. Braaten and R. Jenson, 1:47-63. Philadelphia: Fortress, 1984.

————. *Theology Is for Proclamation*. Minneapolis: Fortress, 1990.

Forell, George. *Understanding the Nicene Creed*. Minneapolis: Fortress, 1965.

Frei, Hans W. *The Identity of Jesus Christ: The Hermeneutical Bases of Dogmatic Theology*. Philadelphia: Fortress, 1975.

————. *Types of Christian Theology*. New Haven: Yale University Press, 1992.

Furlong, Monica. *Christian Uncertainties*. Cambridge, Mass.: Cowley, 1982.

Gardner, W. H., ed. *Poems and Prose of Gerard Manley Hopkins*. Baltimore: Penguin Books, 1966.

Garner, Mary. *The Hidden Souls of Words*. New York: SelectBooks, 2004.

Gaventa, Beverly, and Cynthia Rigby, eds. *The Blessed One: Protestant Perspectives on Mary*. Louisville: Westminster, 2002.

Gerrish, Brian A. *The Old Protestantism and the New*. Chicago: University of Chicago Press, 1982.

Gillespie, Thomas W. *The First Theologians: A Study in Early Christian Prophecy.* Grand Rapids: Eerdmans, 1994.

Godsey, John D. *The Theology of Dietrich Bonhoeffer.* Philadelphia: Westminster, 1960.

Graham, W. Fred. *The Constructive Revolutionary: John Calvin and His Socio-Economic Impact.* Richmond, Va.: John Knox, 1971.

Green, Clifford J. *Bonhoeffer: A Theology of Sociality.* Grand Rapids: Eerdmans, 1999.

Greene, Brian. *The Elegant Universe.* New York: Random House, 2000.

Greene, Graham. *The Power and the Glory.* New York: Viking Press, 1990.

Gregorios, Paulos, William Lazareth, and Nikos Nissiotis, eds. *Does Chalcedon Divide or Unite? Towards a Convergence in Orthodox Christology.* Geneva: World Council of Churches, 1981.

Grillmeier, Aloys. *Christ in Christian Tradition: From the Apostolic Age to Chalcedon.* New York: Sheed and Ward, 1965.

————. *Der Logos am Kreuz.* Munich, 1956.

Grillmeier, A., and H. Bacht, eds. *Das Konzil von Chalkedon.* 3 vols. Würzburg, 1951f.

Gunton, Colin E. *Becoming and Being: The Doctrine of God in Charles Hartshorne and Karl Barth.* New York: Oxford University Press, 1978.

Gutiérrez, Gustavo. *Essential Writings.* Minneapolis: Fortress, 1996.

Hall, John Douglas. *God and Human Suffering: An Exercise in the Theology of the Cross.* Minneapolis: Augsburg, 1986.

————. *Steward.* Grand Rapids: Eerdmans, 1990.

Hardy, E. R., ed. *Christology of the Later Fathers.* Philadelphia: Westminster, 1954.

Hayward, Isabel Carter. *Our Passion for Justice.* New York: Pilgrim Press, 1984.

Hebblethwaite, Brian. *The Essence of Christianity.* London: SPCK, 1996.

Hendry, George S. *The Holy Spirit in Christian Theology.* Philadelphia: Westminster, 1956.

Heron, Alasdair I. C. *The Holy Spirit.* Philadelphia: Westminster, 1983.

Hesselink, John. *On Being Reformed.* New York: Reformed Church Press, 1988.

Hromadke, Josef L. *Impact of History on Theology.* Notre Dame, Ind.: Fides Publishers, 1970.

Hunsinger, Deborah Van Dusen. *Theology and Pastoral Counseling.* Grand Rapids: Eerdmans, 1995.

Hunsinger, George. *Disruptive Grace.* Grand Rapids: Eerdmans, 2000.

————. *How to Read Karl Barth.* New York: Oxford University Press, 1991.

Hunt, George, and John T. McNeill, eds. *Calvinism and the Political Order.* Philadelphia: Westminster, 1965.

Jaeger, Werner. *Early Christianity and Classical Culture.* London: Oxford University Press, 1961.

Jenson, Robert W. *The Triune Identity.* Philadelphia: Fortress, 1982.

————, ed. *Union with Christ: The New Finnish Interpretation of Luther.* Grand Rapids: Eerdmans, 1998.

Johnson, Elizabeth A. "The Incomprehensibility of God and the Image of God Male and Female." *Theological Studies* 45, no. 3 (September 1984): 441-80.

————. *She Who Is.* New York: Crossroad, 1992.

Joint Committee on Worship. *The Worshipbook: Services.* Philadelphia: Westminster, 1970.

Jüngel, Eberhard. *The Doctrine of the Trinity.* Grand Rapids: Eerdmans, 1976.

Jungmann, Josef A. *The Early Liturgy.* Notre Dame, Ind.: University of Notre Dame Press, 1959.

Kasper, Walter. *Faith and the Future.* New York: Crossroad, 1982.

————. *Jesus the Christ.* New York: Paulist, 1976.

Kelly, J. N. D. *The Athanasian Creed.* New York: Harper and Row, 1965.

————. *Early Christian Creeds.* London: Longmans, Green and Co., 1950.

————. *Early Christian Doctrine.* New York: Harper and Bros., 1958.

King, Martin Luther, Jr. *Strength to Love.* Philadelphia: Fortress, 1981.

Kloster, Frederick H. *A Mighty Comfort: The Christian Faith according to the Heidelberg Catechism.* Grand Rapids: CRC Publications, 1990.

Kolfhaus, W. *Christusgemeinshaft bei Johannes Calvin.* Neukirchen: Buchhandlung des Erziehungvereins, 1939.

Lane, Anthony. *Calvin and Bernard of Clairvaux.* Princeton: Princeton Theological Seminary, 1996.

Lathrop, Gordon. *Holy People: A Liturgical Ecclesiology.* Minneapolis: Fortress, 1999.

————. *Holy Things: A Liturgical Theology.* Minneapolis: Fortress, 1993.

Lauber, David Edward. "Towards a Theology of Holy Saturday: Karl Barth and Hans Urs von Balthasar." Ph.D. diss., Princeton Theological Seminary, 1999.

Lee, Philip J. *Against the Protestant Gnostics.* New York: Oxford University Press, 1987.

Lee, Sang Hung. *The Philosophical Theology of Jonathan Edwards.* Princeton: Princeton University Press, 1988.

Lee, Sang Hung, et al., eds. *Faithful Imagining: Essays in Honor of Richard R. Niebuhr.* Atlanta: Scholars, 1995.

Lehmann, Paul. *Ethics in a Christian Context.* New York: Harper and Row, 1963.

Leith, John. *Basic Christian Doctrine.* Louisville: Westminster John Knox, 1993.

————. *An Introduction to the Reformed Tradition.* Atlanta: John Knox, 1977.

————, ed. *Creeds of the Churches.* Garden City, N.Y.: Doubleday, 1963.

Leon-Dufour, Xavier, ed. *Dictionary of Biblical Theology.* 2nd ed. New York: Seabury Press, 1973.

Lindbeck, George. *The Nature of Doctrine.* Philadelphia: Westminster, 1984.

Lochman, Jan Milic. *The Faith We Confess.* Philadelphia: Fortress, 1984.

Loder, James E. *The Knight's Move.* Colorado Springs: Helmers and Howard, 1992.

————. *The Transforming Moment.* San Francisco: Harper and Row, 1981.

Lossky, Vladimir. *In the Image and Likeness of God.* New York: St. Vladimir's Seminary Press, 1974.

MacGregor, Geddes. *Corpus Christi.* Philadelphia: Westminster, 1959.

————. *The Nicene Creed Illumined by Modern Thought.* Grand Rapids: Eerdmans, 1980.

Maury, Pierre. *Predestination . . . with Foreword by Karl Barth.* Richmond, Va.: John Knox, 1960.

Mauser, Ulrich W. *Gottesbild und Menschwerdung: Eine Untersuchung zur Einheit des Alten und Neuen Testaments.* Tübingen: Mohr, 1971.

Maxwell, William D. *An Outline of Christian Worship: Its Development and Forms.* London: Oxford University Press, 1952.

McCormack, Bruce L. *For Us and Our Salvation: Incarnation and Atonement in the Reformed Tradition.* Studies in Reformed Theology and History. Princeton: Princeton Theological Seminary, 1993.

————. *Karl Barth's Critically Realistic Dialectical Theology: Its Genesis and Development, 1909-1936.* Oxford: Clarendon, 1995.

McGrath, Alister. *Iustitia Dei: A History of the Christian Doctrine of Justification.* New York: Cambridge University Press, 1998.

————. *Luther's Theology of the Cross.* Oxford: Blackwell, 1985.

McKelway, Alexander J. *The Freedom of God and Human Liberation.* London: SCM, 1990.

————. "The Logic of Faith." In *Toward the Future of Reformed Theology,* edited by David Willis and Michael Welker. Grand Rapids: Eerdmans, 1999.

————. *The Systematic Theology of Paul Tillich.* Richmond, Va.: John Knox, 1964.

McKim, Donald K., ed. *Encyclopedia of the Reformed Faith.* Louisville: Westminster John Knox, 1992.

McNeill, John T. *The History and Character of Calvinism.* New York: Oxford University Press, 1954.

McWilliam, Joan, ed. *Augustine: From Rhetor to Theologian.* Waterloo, Ont.: Wilfrid Laurier University Press, 1992.

Melville, Herman. *Moby Dick.* New York: Oxford University Press, 1947.

Menninger, Karl. *The Vital Balance.* New York: Viking Press, 1963.

———. *Whatever Happened to Sin?* New York: Hawthorne, 1973.

Meyendorf, John. *Catholicity and the Church.* Crestwood, N.Y.: St. Vladimir's Seminary Press, 1983.

———. *Christ in Eastern Christian Thought.* 1969.

———. *St. Gregory Palamas and Orthodox Spirituality.* New York: St. Vladimir's Seminary Press, 1974.

Meyer, Harding, and Lukas Vischer, eds. *Growth in Agreement: Reports and Agreed Statements of Ecumenical Conversations on a World Level.* New York: Paulist, 1984.

Micks, Marianne. *Loving the Questions* [on the Nicene Creed]. Cambridge, Mass.: Cowley, 1993.

———. *Our Search for Identity: Humanity in the Image of God.* Philadelphia: Fortress, 1982.

Migliore, Daniel. *Faith Seeking Understanding: An Introduction to Christian Theology.* Grand Rapids: Eerdmans, 1991.

Miller, Patrick D. *Interpreting the Psalms.* Philadelphia: Fortress, 1986.

Minear, Paul S. *Christians and the New Creation: Genesis Motifs in the New Testament.* Louisville: Westminster John Knox, 1994.

Mitchell, Louis. *Jonathan Edwards on the Experience of Beauty.* Princeton: Princeton Theological Seminary, 2003.

Moltmann, Jürgen. *The Crucified God.* New York: Harper and Row, 1974.

———. *God in Creation.* San Francisco: Harper and Row, 1985.

———. "Liberation in the Light of Hope." In *The Context of Contemporary Theology: Essays in Honor of Paul Lehmann,* edited by Alexander J. McKelway and E. David Willis, pp. 127-54. Atlanta: John Knox, 1974.

———. *Theology of Hope.* New York: Harper and Row, 1967.

Morimoto, Anri. *Jonathan Edwards and the Catholic Vision of Salvation.* University Park: Pennsylvania State University Press, 1995.

"Moscow Statement Agreed by the Anglo-Orthodox Joint Doctrinal Commission." 1976. London: SPCK, 1977.

Muilenberg, James. *The Way of Israel: Biblical Faith and Ethics.* New York: Harper and Row, 1961.

Nevin, John W. *The Mystical Presence and Other Writings on the Eucharist.* Lancaster Series on the Mercersberg Theology, edited by Bard Thompson and George H. Bricker, vol. 4. Philadelphia: United Church, 1966.

Niebuhr, H. Richard. *Christ and Culture.* New York: Harper Torchbooks, 1956.

———. *The Responsible Self.* New York: Harper and Row, 1963.

Niebuhr, Reinhold. *The Nature and Destiny of Man.* New York: Charles Scribner's Sons, 1955.

Noth, Martin. "The 'Representation' of the Old Testament in Proclamation." In *Essays on Old Testament Hermeneutics,* edited by Claus Westermann and James Luther Mays, pp. 76-88. Richmond, Va.: John Knox, 1963.

Oberman, Heiko A. *Initia Calvini: The Matrix of Calvin's Reformation.* Amsterdam: Koninklijke Nederlandse Akademie van Wetenschappen, 1991.

————. *Luther: Man between God and the Devil.* New Haven: Yale University Press, 1989.

O'Connor, Flannery. *The Habit of Being.* New York: Farrar, Straus and Giroux, 1979.

————. *Three: "Wise Blood," "A Good Man Is Hard to Find," "The Violent Bear It Away."* New York: New American Library, 1962.

Osterhaven, M. Eugene. *The Spirit of the Reformed Tradition.* Grand Rapids: Eerdmans, 1971.

Pannenberg, Wolfhart. *Faith and Reality.* Philadelphia: Westminster, 1977.

————. *The Idea of God and Human Freedom.* Philadelphia: Westminster, 1973.

Partee, Charles. "Calvin's Central Dogma Again." *Calvin Studies,* Papers of the 1986 Davidson Colloquium, edited by J. Leith, Union Theological Seminary, Richmond, Va., pp. 39-46.

Pasztor, Janos Dezso. *Leonard Ragaz: Pioneer Social Theologian.* New York, 1973.

Pattison, Bonnie L. Goding. "The Concept of Poverty in Calvin's Christology and Its Influence on His Doctrine of the Christian Life and the Church." Ph.D. diss., Princeton Theological Seminary, 1997.

Pegis, Anton, ed. *Introduction to St. Thomas Aquinas.* New York: Random House, Modern Library, 1948.

Pelikan, Jaroslav. *Bach among the Theologians.* Philadelphia: Fortress, 1986.

————. *The Christian Tradition.* Vol. 1, *The Emergence of the Catholic Tradition (100-600).* Chicago: University of Chicago Press, 1971.

————. *Imago Dei: The Byzantine Apologia for Icons.* Washington, D.C.: National Gallery of Art, 1990.

Placher, William C. *The Domestication of Transcendence.* Louisville: Westminster John Knox, 1996.

————. *A History of Christian Theology.* Philadelphia: Westminster, 1983.

————. *Narratives of a Vulnerable God: Christ, Theology, and Scripture.* Louisville: Westminster John Knox, 1994.

————. *Unapologetic Theology: A Christian Voice in a Pluralistic Conversation.* Louisville: Westminster John Knox, 1989.

————. "The Vulnerability of God." In *Toward the Future of Reformed Theology,* edited by D. Willis and M. Welker. Grand Rapids: Eerdmans, 1999.

————, ed. *Essentials of Christian Theology*. Louisville: Westminster John Knox, 2003.

Placher, William C., and David Willis-Watkins. *Belonging to God: A Commentary on "A Brief Statement of Faith."* Louisville: Westminster John Knox, 1992.

Plantinga, Cornelius, Jr. *Trinity, Incarnation, and Atonement*. Notre Dame, Ind.: University of Notre Dame Press, 1989.

Polkinghorne, John. *Quarks, Chaos, and Christianity*. London: Triangle, 1994.

Polkinghorne, John, and Michael Welker, eds. *The End of the World and the Ends of God*. Harrisburg, Pa.: Trinity, 2000.

Presbyterian Church U.S.A. *The Constitution, Part I, Book of Confessions*. Louisville: Office of the General Assembly, 1994.

Prestige, G. L. *God in Patristic Thought*. London: SPCK, 1952.

Quasten, Johannes. *Patrology*. Vol. 3. Westminster, Md.: Newman, 1960.

Rahner, Karl. *The Trinity*. London: Herder, 1970.

Ricoeur, Paul. *The Conflict of Interpretations*. Evanston, Ill.: Northwestern University Press, 1974.

Rigby, Cynthia L. "The Real Word Really Became Flesh: Karl Barth's Contribution to a Feminist Incarnational Christology." Ph.D. diss., Princeton Theological Seminary, 1998.

Sakenfeld, Katharine Doob. *Faithfulness in Action*. Philadelphia: Fortress, 1985.

Sauter, Gerhard. *The Question of Meaning*. Grand Rapids: Eerdmans, 1995.

Schaff, Philip. *Creeds of Christendom*. Grand Rapids: Baker, 1966.

Schillebeeckx, E. *Christ the Sacrament of the Encounter with God*. New York: Sheed and Ward, 1963.

Schmemann, Alexander. *I Believe . . .* Crestwood, N.Y.: St. Vladimir's Seminary Press, 1995.

————. *Introduction to Liturgical Theology*. Crestwood, N.Y.: St. Vladimir's Seminary Press, 1986.

Seitz, Christopher, ed. *Nicene Christianity*. Grand Rapids: Brazos, 2001.

Smedes, Lewis B. *A Pretty Good Person*. San Francisco: Harper and Row, 1990.

Sonderegger, Katherine. *That Jesus Christ Was Born a Jew: Karl Barth's Doctrine of Israel*. University Park: Pennsylvania State University Press, 1992.

Stackhouse, Max L. *Creeds, Society, and Human Rights*. Grand Rapids: Eerdmans, 1984.

Stead, Christopher. *Divine Substance*. Oxford: Clarendon, 1977.

Stringfellow, William. *Free in Obedience*. New York: Seabury Press, 1964.

Stuperich, Robert. *Melanchthon*. Philadelphia: Westminster, 1965.

Taylor, Barbara Brown. *The Luminous Web: Essays on Science and Religion*. Cambridge, Mass.: Cowley, 2000.

Terrien, Samuel. *The Elusive Presence: The Heart of Biblical Theology.* San Francisco: Harper and Row, 1978.

Tillich, Paul. *Systematic Theology.* 3 vols. Chicago: University of Chicago Press, 1951-63.

Torrance, Iain. *Christology after Chalcedon: Severus of Antioch and Sergius the Monophysite.* Norwich: Canterbury Press, 1988.

Torrance, Iain, and Bryan Spinks, eds. *To Glorify God: Essays on Modern Reformed Liturgy.* Edinburgh: T. & T. Clark, 1999.

Torrance, James B. "The Vicarious Humanity of Christ." In *The Incarnation,* edited by Thomas F. Torrance, chap. 6. Edinburgh: Handsel Press, 1981.

Torrance, Thomas F. *Belief in Science and in Christian Life: The Relevance of Michael Polanyi's Thought for Christian Faith and Life.* Edinburgh: Handsel Press, 1980.

———. *The Christian Doctrine of God: One Being, Three Persons.* Edinburgh: T. & T. Clark, 1996.

———. *Reality and Scientific Theology.* Edinburgh: Scottish Academic Press, 1985.

———. *Royal Priesthood.* Edinburgh: Oliver and Boyd, 1955.

———. *Space, Time, and the Incarnation.* London: Oxford University Press, 1969.

———. *Space, Time, and the Resurrection.* Grand Rapids: Eerdmans, 1976.

———, ed. *The Incarnation: Ecumenical Studies in the Nicene-Constantinopolitan Creed.* Edinburgh: Handsel Press, 1981.

Van Dyk, Leanne. *Believing in Jesus Christ.* Louisville: Geneva Press, 2002.

———. *The Desire of Divine Love: John McLeod Campbell's Doctrine of the Atonement.* New York: P. Lang, 1995.

———. "Toward a New Typology of Reformed Doctrines of Atonement." In *Toward the Future of Reformed Theology,* edited by D. Willis and M. Welker, pp. 225-38. Grand Rapids: Eerdmans, 1999.

Vischer, Lukas. "Church: Mother of Believers." In *Toward the Future of Reformed Theology,* edited by D. Willis and M. Welker. Grand Rapids: Eerdmans, 1999.

———, ed. *Reformed Witness Today: A Collection of Confessions and Statements of Faith Issued by Reformed Churches.* Bern: Evangelische Arbeitsstelle Oekumene Schweiz, 1982.

Volf, Miroslav. *After Our Likeness: The Church as the Image of the Trinity.* Grand Rapids: Eerdmans, 1998.

———. "Theology, Meaning and Power: A Conversation with George Lindbeck on Theology and the Nature of Christian Difference." In *The Nature of Confession,* edited by Timothy R. Phillips and Dennis L. Okholm, pp. 45-56. Downers Grove, Ill.: InterVarsity, 1996.

Wainwright, Geoffrey. *Doxology.* New York: Oxford University Press, 1980.

Webster, John. *Barth's Ethics of Reconciliation*. Cambridge: Cambridge University Press, 1995.

————. *Holiness*. Grand Rapids: Eerdmans, 2003.

Welker, Michael. *God the Spirit*. Minneapolis: Fortress, 1994.

————. *What Happens in Holy Communion?* Grand Rapids: Eerdmans, 2000.

Wesley, John. *Sermons on Several Occasions*. Rev. ed. London: Epworth, 1946.

Wilder, Amos. *Theopoetic*. Philadelphia: Fortress, 1976.

Willis, David. *Calvin's Catholic Christology*. Leiden: Brill, 1966.

————. *Notes on the Holiness of God*. Grand Rapids: Eerdmans, 2002.

————. "Proclaiming Liberation for the Earth's Sake." In *For Creation's Sake*, edited by Dieter T. Hessel, pp. 55-70. Philadelphia: Geneva Press, 1985.

————. *The Second Commandment and Church Reform: The Colloquy of St. Germain-en-Laye, 1562*. Princeton: Princeton Theological Seminary, 1994.

————. "The Steadfastness of the Holy Spirit." In *Evangelism in the Reformed Tradition*, edited by Arnold B. Lovell, pp. 85-95. Decatur, Ga.: CTS Press, 1990.

————. "Women's Ordination: Can the Church Be Catholic without It?" In *Women, Gender, and Christian Community*, edited by Jane Dempsey Douglass and James F. Kay, pp. 82-91. Louisville: Westminster John Knox, 1997.

————, ed. *Baptism: Decision and Growth*. Philadelphia: Office of the General Assembly, 1972.

Willis, David, and Michael Welker, eds. *Toward the Future of Reformed Theology*. Grand Rapids: Eerdmans, 1999.

Wilmore, Gayraud S., and James H. Cone, eds. *Black Theology: A Documentary History, 1966-1979*. Maryknoll, N.Y.: Orbis, 1979.

Wingren, Gustaf. *Man and the Incarnation: A Study of the Biblical Theology of Irenaeus*. Philadelphia: Muhlenberg, 1959.

Wolf, Hans Walter. *Anthropology of the Old Testament*. Philadelphia: Fortress, 1974.

Zimmerli, Walther. "Promise and Fulfillment." In *Essays on Old Testament Hermeneutics*, edited by Claus Westermann and James Luther Mays, pp. 89-122. Richmond, Va.: John Knox, 1963.

Zizioulas, John. *Being as Communion: Studies in Personhood and the Church*. Crestwood, N.Y.: St. Valdimir's Seminary Press, 1985.

Index

✛   ✛

Abbey Dore, 3
Abelard, 88
Accommodation: and God's self-accommodation, 45; and reciprocal love, 45; of the Word, 118-19. *See also* Revelation
Accountability: and betrayal, 114-17; judgment of the living and the dead, 164
Aesthetics, 16, 73-75
Allen, Diogenes, 7
Almighty: corrected senses of, 44-45. *See also* Sovereignty
Amazement, 21. *See also* Awe; Wonder
Analogy, 3, 40-46, 70, 163
Angels, 119
Anselm of Canterbury, 88
Apollinaris, 54, 75
Apostles' Creed, 7
Anderson, Bernhard, 47
Arius, 70-71
Architecture, 2
Assumption of humanity, 75, 94-

96. *See also* Gregory Nazianzus; Incarnation; Jesus Christ
Assurance of pardon, 6, 92
Athanasian Creed, 11
Athanasius, 75, 88
Atonement, 87-91; multitude of biblical images for, 87-91; propitiation and false scandal, 91-96; theories of, 87-96. *See also* Reconciliation; Redemption
Augustine, 57-58, 106, 132
Aulen, Gustav, 88
Awe, 12, 21, 28, 51. *See also* Amazement; Delight; Wonder

Bach, Johann Sebastian, 164
Baptism, 4; and Christening, 8; and forgiveness of sin, 116-17; and repentance, 114-17
Barmen Declaration, 119
Barth, Karl, 46, 47, 88, 103, 105, 160
Believing, 19-36; believing about and believing in, 79; believing that and believing in, 20, 44; and symbols, 78. *See also* Faith

Taylor, Barbara Brown, 39
Teresa of Avila, St., 132
Thomas Aquinas, 35, 132
Tillich, Paul, 2, 17-18, 62
Tolerance, 16. *See also* Humility
Tolkien, J. R. R., 27
Torrance, Iain, 5, 78n.9
Torrance, Thomas F., x
Trinity, 9, 103-4. *See also* God

Union: of believers and Christ, 78;
    mystical body, 66; of two na-
    tures, 75-78

Van Dyk, Leanne, 6in.2, 88n.2
Vischer, Lukas, 11, 26
Volf, Miroslav, 17
Vuillard, Edouard, 128

Welker, Michael, 20, 39, 45, 103
Williams, George H., 9
Wilder, Amos, 58n.15
Willis, Ann, 141n.13
Willis, David, 2, 20, 45, 76, 153
Wonder, 12. *See also* Amazement;
    Awe
Word, x; eternal Word Jesus
    Christ, 4, 17-18, 64; and Holy
    Spirit, 74-75; proclaimed Word,
    5; singular Word and plural
    words, 67; the twice begetting
    of, 65-70; written Word, 4
Worship, 4-6

Zen, 12
Zinzendorfians, 132n.3